Huston-Tillotson University
Research Journal

Second Edition

authorHOUSE®

AuthorHouse™
1663 Liberty Drive, Suite 200
Bloomington, IN 47403
www.authorhouse.com
Phone: 1-800-839-8640

First published by AuthorHouse 8/4/2009

ISBN: 978-1-4389-7412-5 (e)
ISBN: 978-1-4389-7413-2 (sc)

Library of Congress Control Number: 2009905102

Printed in the United States of America
Bloomington, Indiana

This book is printed on acid-free paper.

THE SECOND EDITION OF THE HUSTON-TILLOTSON UNIVERSITY RESEARCH JOURNAL has the goal of disseminating research presentations prepared and presented by Huston-Tillotson University students at the Annual Huston-Tillotson University Student Research Day (April 24, 2007 and April 22 2008).

THE HUSTON-TILLOTSON UNIVERSITY RESEARCH JOURNAL is published annually for Huston-Tillotson University, 900 Chicon Street, Austin, Texas 78702

Contents

LETTER FROM THE PRESIDENT

The second and third Huston-Tillotson (HT) Research Days 2007-08 and this student research publication (2nd edition) continue the University's reinvigoration of its historical legacy of empirical investigation that was begun with the inaugural Huston-Tillotson Research Day 2006 and its accompanying Inaugural Huston-Tillotson University Research Journal. These current works, as did those in the previous edition, continue to exemplify HT's historical distinction for promoting scientific inquiry and research.

Additionally, these student researchers go beyond discovery and extend social commentary and poignant recommendations for the improvement of humanity based on their research findings. These thought provoking works challenged society in terms of its obligation to: children at risk for mental disorder (Alvarez); adolescent males who are susceptible to delinquency (Blackmon); abused teens and young women (Hernandez); the mentally ill (Garza); the homeless (Ormsby); future generations (Speed and Tavernier); martyrs from its past (Morris); the environment (Northcote); education (Zea-Hernandez); and health (Rancier and Brinkley).

Enhancing the quality of the human condition and life is a thematic thread that connects this research, which further complements the legacy of HT. The University was born out of a confluence of forces that demanded education as a basic human right for what was at that time our most vulnerable population post slavery. An outgrowth of this is the distinction that HT holds as the oldest institution of higher education in Central Texas, with a mission that has remained consistent with the themes of this excellent research produced by our students.

Larry L. Earvin, Ph.D.
President and CEO

FOREWORD

The research presented at the Second and Third Huston-Tillotson University (HT) Research Days in 2007 and 2008 has been published in this combined edition of the Huston-Tillotson University Research Journal. The journal continues to advance the University's goal to enhance student learning through research.

A broad range of areas that address the role of environment on the human condition are included in this edition, such as: behavior modification and cognitive intervention with at-risk children (Alvarez) and adolescents (Blackmon); the impact of trauma and abuse on the self esteem of females (Hernandez); social and human rights support of the mentally ill (Garza) and homeless (Ormsby); the effects of global warming (Northcote); the health effects of cigarettes (Rancier); classroom content's effect on learning (Zea-Hernandez); psycho-socio-historical-political influences on intergenerational differences in development (Speed and Tavernier); and the importance of knowing our history in order to understand our present (Morris).

These contributors have met the challenge of the high standard of scholarship set forth by the student researchers in the inaugural edition. They are to be commended highly for maintaining the bar, which must be continued by the next student contributors.

Joseph Jones, Jr. Ph.D.
Dean, College of Arts and Sciences

I. Current Research at HT (Papers)

Bipolar Disorder in Adolescents: A Case Analysis

Adam Alvarez
Junior, Psychology

(Dr. Debra L. Murphy, Major Advisor for Psychology)

Abstract

The prevalence and incidence of bipolar disorder (BPD) diagnoses in children and adolescents has increased. The purpose of this report is to educate parents, those affected with the disease, as well as, educators and psychological professionals about this severe mental disease. This research examined case studies in order to delineate recognizable symptoms. The study also reviewed recommended treatment methods. The research literature that was reviewed indicated that customizable therapeutic programs and consistent medication administration are at the forefront of a positive treatment program. The five case studies of children between seven and ten years of age were observed in a residential treatment center over a month with behavioral manifestations and changes noted. The increased rates of BPD adolescents should raise a red flag that calls for the need to increase awareness and knowledge about BPD and the need for timely implementation of recommended therapeutic interventions. Findings were consistent with the importance of understanding symptoms and behaviors associated with the disease in order to provide early intervention. This may provide this population with better coping strategies that can possibly prevent them from developing into unstable adults.

Introduction

The recognition of mental disorders in children at earlier ages can allow for therapeutic interventions that may be closer to onset and therefore possibly more effective in the prevention of the worsening of the disorder into the teen and adult years. Further, the education of parents and educators about the warning signs and symptoms can serve to involve them in the process of monitoring and early intervention/prevention. According to the *Diagnostic and Statistical Manual of Mental Disorders IV* (Tomb, 1995) BPD is described as follows:

It involves major depression (MD) with episodes of manic or hypo-manic states which can be uncontrolled and psychotic. It is a genetic disorder and a recurrent illness. Clients may exhibit contrasting symptoms simultaneously. A total of twenty percent ((20%) of clients have hallucinations and or delusions.

Since it is certain that BPD is a genetic disease, the tendency for it to be passed down to the affected parent's offspring is very high. According to Rabinowitz and Yang (1999), "The tendency for the onset of a genetic disease to

3

occur at progressively earlier ages, or with greater severity, in successive generations is known as 'anticipation'." There is a much recognized pattern of parents having MD symptoms and their children exhibiting the same. Due to the fact that BPD disorder is a genetic disease, affected parents should consider having their children tested by doctors who specialize in this area. Follow up research indicates a second set of results from phenotype studies that showed increased evidence of a linkage between BPD and the twelfth chromosome.

A question that has arisen is whether or not the children of affected parents are exhibiting symptoms at earlier age onset because they are modeling what they see at home, or is it because the symptoms are genuine and psychologically uncontrolled. The research reviewed indicated that once the child reaches a point where his behavior is unmanageable to the parents, he/she is admitted to an inpatient program. It has been questioned whether or not the "rates of psychosis may appear higher among inpatient subjects than outpatient subjects" (Patel, 2006). The study examined the manic symptoms of the subjects which, in some cases, led to a restraint or seclusion due to uncontrollable aggressiveness. The hypothesis in this research explored whether or not the therapeutic milieu contributed to or reduced episodes of negative mania, and if occurrences of interventions (physical holds and seclusions) for subjects may have been directly related to the occurrence of their peers' interventions and negative behavior.

Further, the literature has found that there seems to be a potential effect on the surrounding clients when another peer reaches a point of extremely escalating negative behavior. The validity of the environmental effect on psychotic behavior is challenged in Krout's analysis of Dunham's ecology of functional psychosis premise and views the "cause of psychosis as being a combination of external factors and an inner constellation" (Krout, 1938).

The environmental situations around the client are highly likely to cause a change in mood. As the number of children diagnosed with BPD rises, it is important for people to understand the sociological context from which they come. In comparing symptom profiles of adolescents with BPD, the African American group exhibited more psychotic features and auditory hallucinations than its white cohort (Patel, Delbello, Strakowski, 2006). Patel's study states there may be a higher number of misdiagnoses at a later age (i.e., schizophrenia).

The justification of this research study was to see if grouping similarly aged children with similar diagnoses of BPD is the most beneficial therapeutic environment. Structure in the child's programming is provided by the schedule adherence models. From an existentialistic approach to adolescent development, the child must be given freedom with responsibility. In other words, to have them fully adhere to schedules overseen by an authoritative figure, it may take away from their learning through experience. The child, with guidance, should be allowed to learn through experiences of his own, followed by an evaluation of whether or not the problem solving techniques used were acceptable. The child may become at risk for developing distorted views imposed on him by a biased adult (Fitzgerald, 2005). Again, is the therapeutic environment helping or hurting? The research was done to observe not only the client behavior, but the causes of the behavior. Changes in the child's behavior were also examined. Each case study is different, so there will be variations in the behavioral changes, with some showing a major positive change and others demonstrating a regression or no change at all.

In interviewing three therapists on their therapeutic approaches, they all respond the same. With the older kids (ten years of age and older) they tend to use cognitive therapy approaches, as well as, family systems therapy. It is commonly accepted in the field that behavioral and play therapy are more conducive to younger children, as they respond better to it. In the direct contact with the clients, it is clear that the behavioral approach is very effective, In other words, it is simple: this action equals this consequence. One other valuable approach used in the study is the Adlerian approach which is designed to illuminate personal strengths and help to recognize that they are in charge of their own lives and to provide them with the encouragement that they need to make different choices based on new understanding (Corey, 2006). Since children who have mood disorders often use their past to predict how they act in the present, it is imperative that they receive the praise and encouragement they deserve when the positive change in behavior occurs. To further assist in controlling and changing the child's behavior, the relationship with the surrounding adults and mentors is crucial. Their development and

behavioral learning is related to their own self worth. "These relationships or 'sense of connections' with others are key to their psychological well-being and growth fostering" (Gibson and Jefferson, 2006).

In regard to the changing moods, it is questionable whether or not their goals may change (Mestas and Urdan, 2006). Staying involved with the children and maintaining constant communication, especially about what their goals are and what they *really want*, helps to understand what state of mind the child is in. Mestas and Urdan (2006) also noted that, "The child's goals must be stated in his/her own words." It is very helpful for them to understand society's expectations of acceptable behavior. Because psychotic symptoms in mania can produce a skewed perception of reality, it must be clearly engrained in the child's mind how they should act. It is said that Virginia Woolf accredited her great creativity to her madness (Caramagno, 1998). She suffered and admitted that she was crazy; however she was able to harness the creative side. Despite her suicide attempts, she had a way of coping with some of her manic episodes. It is clear that some of the observed children may grow up and have similar thoughts, but the goal of treatment is to improve available coping skills. When something becomes a habit, the body and mind function automatically, and without much thought. The prevalence of fighting and weapon use is substantially and significantly elevated among people diagnosed with psychotic and bipolar disorders. The prevailing research in the field shows that people with these diagnoses are more likely to engage in violent behavior than those who do not have the diagnosis (three to nine times more likely). All of the children in this study have shown acts of aggression and lack of impulse control. This paper will also discuss the changes in behavior of the studied clients and what possible causes are related. If the child can learn bad habits of poor impulse control along with verbal and physical aggression, can they form new habits to respond more positively and self controlled?

Method

The collection of the data for this study was through the observation of case studies. Those observed were ages seven to ten years of age and the sample size was five. The subject's daily records of their behavior, medications, and therapeutic sessions were also examined. In BPD there is a manic phase, one of elated and hyperactive presence, and also a depressive phase, which is characterized by extreme lows and a sense of helplessness. The goal of this study was to observe and document the extent to which behavioral interactions of the clients with each other and the author/researcher of this paper might be a function of the medication changes and/or customized therapeutic treatment plans (which the author/researcher assisted with determining).

The setting was a behavioral treatment center for children (the name and location will not be cited in order to protect the confidentiality of the clients). The children were housed in one area with others in the same age range and provided a schedule to follow. There was data recorded on a daily basis of the clients' overall demeanor and behavior.

The data analyses and observations included statistical comparisons, noted behavioral modification methods, how the residents reacted to peers and situations, as well as, the coping mechanisms used by the residents. The time span was over one month at forty hours per week with continuity of care and consistent schedule adherence. Each case study was different and the data presented provided an overall view of the client's progression or regression. Personal testimonials about residents' perceptions of medication and treatment effectiveness were also documented.

The inclusion of both quantitative and qualitative data were used to provide a more complete understanding of how children affected with BPD live, what treatments are available, and how to assist them by teaching them coping strategies and providing them with the appropriate medication regime.

Case Studies

The case studies included five adolescent males between ages seven and ten years of age. Due to confidentiality issues, randomly chosen pseudo names were used to identify each. Each of the clients had been diagnosed primarily, with BPD and other mental disorders, which included Oppositional Defiant Disorder (ODD), Asperger's Syndrome, Attention Deficit Hyperactivity Disorder (ADHD), and attachment disorders.

ODD is characterized by the child exhibiting *the terrible two's* attitude, even through adolescence and is often accompanied with a diagnosis of ADHD. Asperger's syndrome is a developmental disorder in which people have difficulties understanding how to socially interact. With attachment disorders, children generally did not bond, attach, or trust their mothers during the first three years of life. Each of these mental disorders adds to what the primary mood disorder is, and makes it very difficult for the child to understand and empathize.

For each case study, data were analyzed which reflected certain behavioral manifestations (i.e. physical aggression, verbal outbursts, property destruction, and oppositional behavior) as well as emergency interventions (physical holds and seclusions). Also, a critical incident was documented that included: the description of a highly recognized negative behavior, the resident's and staff's interpretation of its cause, the problem it presented, the intervention technique that was used, and the resolution.

The cases represented a convenience sample based on their availability to the researcher/observer who interacted with them daily. Observations confirmed that there was adequate staff to resident interaction and continuity of care, which the research literature suggests provide the greatest results in behavior therapy; therefore the outcomes of this study cannot be attributed to any deficiencies in the aforementioned areas. With the exception of internal room and roommate changes, the cases in the study were primarily exposed to each, so the behavioral outcomes could not be accounted for by new admissions, or environmental changes. The presence of BPD in these reported children allowed for a positive identification of symptoms observed and noted.

The cases were interviewed via group therapy sessions about the following: their feelings for the current day, both before and after medication administration; their goals and how peers and staff can assist them; and their self recommendations for having a positive day. For example, in group, Client W remarked, "If I get mad, I would like to take a break in my room and to have staff come talk to me. I really don't want any of my peers trying to calm me down." It made handling situations easier when the child suggested something, in front of his peers and staff that will work positively for him.

Client B

Client B had a history of familial instability. He had been diagnosed with Asperger's disease, BPD, and ODD. He was generally characterized as energetic, socially capable, when he wanted to be, and had an overall presence of well being. He had a brother who still lived at home with his foster mom. During treatment he failed to maintain a higher level, with regard to the token economy system, and consistently received consequences for major negative behavior. The ODD was observed daily, almost hourly. His 243 noted acts fell below the monthly total of 276.8. His defiant behavior was most noted when staff attempted to redirect him back to his designated area, like his room, the social room for group, or the cafeteria for dinner. Once the child reached a state of complete agitation he was difficult to calm down and avoided all social interaction. He became completely nonverbal and made grunting and growling noises, followed by extreme aggressiveness (47 aggressive acts per month), which included throwing objects, slamming his door, and yelling and attacking those nearby. Once the intervention took place (physical hold, seclusion, or verbal processing), he returned to an elated state, followed by apologies and close positive physical interaction. In one critical incident, he had trouble getting along with a peer, when the group lined up for dinner. He horse played and had trouble controlling his impulses. He spat upon his peer's head and then pretended to punch him in the face. This was similar to his elated and manic states. As the entire group was sent back to their rooms for feeding into his negativity, he began to go into a rage. He kicked people and had to be taken to the timeout room. About 15 minutes after, he calmed down and was deeply apologetic towards his peers and staff. He offered to shower first, and completed everyone's dorm job on his own. During his manic phase, he cleaned until everything looked perfect and he wanted to do it alone because he felt that others would just get in his way.

Client A

Client A had a history that included coming from a family that traveled a lot, and was diagnosed with BPD, ODD and ADHD. He had major trouble with his mood swings. He had attacked his infant sister numerous times, aggressively bitten his mother in the face, and grabbed his elderly neighbor's cane and hit him repeatedly in the legs with it. His mother also reported that he was admitted after he attacked the cops who came to assist his pregnant mother during a major struggle. Client A was usually in a manic state around the clock, evidenced by his wide open eyes and giddy smile. During groups he reported, "I feel happy, happy, happy,

and excited." Upon observation, this exclamation appeared true. He had major challenges staying still and presented, in his restlessness, an overly hyper state and tended to invade peers' boundaries, playing way too rough, and speaking very loudly. He was observed spinning around in circles, speaking gibberish, and laughing as if he were being tickled. His aggressive acts were usually a result of a peer becoming agitated by his annoying and *in your face* attitude. It has been noted that he had more physical acts of aggression than his peers (57). On one occasion a peer became so upset at Client A's attempts to wrestle and play rough that he told the staff and the boys were separated. Client A became furious and thought, irrationally, that his peer did not like him. He ran back into the room and began choking his peer while at the same time kicking him. He was immediately physically held for his aggression. Once he was physically held he usually exerted so much energy that the rest of the day he was calm and able to complete his consequential written tasks very quickly. He exuded more of a depressive state afterward and he told me that he felt that nobody liked him. He cycled very quickly throughout the day, but once he reached the point of getting held, secluded or sent to timeout, he showed more controlled behavior.

Client W

Client W had a history of familial instability. He was diagnosed with BPD and ADHD. He usually presented himself as feeling happy during groups, and was very social. He was well liked by everyone around him and he could be extremely helpful in peer to peer interaction as a form of processing when others were agitated. Client W was competitive and his acts of aggression were usually attributed to not being first in line, or losing at an activity. Verbal aggressive acts mostly included racial slurs and cursing while using obscene gestures. He was noted as having the ability to regain composure very quickly, almost instantly. In some cases when he was provoked by peers, because of his small stature and baby-like speech, he became physically aggressive. It was recently noted that after he was confronted by a peer, he bit his peer in the face, leaving an open wound. About ninety percent (90%) of the time, he acted out, and he followed up with half an hour of crying and depressive moods. He also stated, "I am always a bad boy; my brain keeps making me do bad things. Nobody likes me and my mom doesn't even want me."

Client J

Client J was diagnosed with BPD, ODD, and attachment disorder. He is noted in the data as having the highest incidents of defiant behavior (404). He had major mood swings that were presented in major states of helplessness versus his outgoing and friendly normal state. During the day he tended to program more positively than in the evening. Early in the morning was extremely challenging for him as was bedtime. His major goals in treatment were to treat others with respect and to get his needs met in an appropriate way. His acts of verbal and physical aggression, as well as, sexually acting out were mostly observed in the morning or evening. On more than one occasion he became so agitated that

he urinated on the floors in hopes that the staff or peers would walk in it. He had also, repeatedly, smeared feces on the walls and defecated on the floor, followed by throwing it on the ceiling. He stated, "I know that the staff has to help me clean the mess up, so that's how I get back at them."

Client M

Client M was diagnosed with BPD and ODD. He was sent to treatment by his mother (who was also in and out of treatment centers) after he tried to drown her in the pool when she told him it was time to get out. It is reported that he had the second highest number of verbal incidents in the group. His moods tended to be very unstable during the day. He was constantly putting blame on others, provoking others and showing bad boundaries. He very rarely showed any manic symptoms during the day, but he was very energetic and outspoken. He almost always had trouble sleeping and was the last one to fall asleep, about 2 hours after bedtime. On one occasion he was observed getting extremely agitated over a seemingly unfair consequence. He was not taking responsibility for his aggressive actions toward a peer at activity time and began throwing his shoes at the staff, and scratched and attempted to bite them. He refused to calm down and was restrained for almost half an hour, which ceased once he was given a shot of Zyprexa for his aggression.

Data Collection

The data were primarily collected through notes and number tracking after the incidents occurred. The numbers tallied were combined with those on the earlier shifts, when the researcher/observer was not present. After observing the behavior, it was noted on the client's chart. The clients remained unaware of the amount of behaviors that were noted. So, as the numbers were gathered, the therapeutic approach may have changed depending on what behaviors were noted. For example, if a client showed major signs of aggression and required emergency interventions, his therapy may be modified to help him find positive coping skills. The data collected were analyzed and charted to see what behaviors were most prevalent. The data were also analyzed to observe trends that may have occurred during the four week span. Most of the children reported a sense of well being at the day community group time, as well as, feeling either happy or sad. They seemed to lack the knowledge of other possible feelings besides happy, sad or energetic. Because of this, not much data were collected on their feelings; however it was more aptly noted in their behaviors. The primary behaviors noted were physically aggressive acts, verbal outbursts, oppositional behavior and interventions.

Statistics

Once the data collection was complete, the numbers were totaled, and a mean was computed. There were some trends noted and correlations made from the data that was analyzed. The conventional data collection method was used, for example, a behavior was recognized (for example cursing or hitting) and was immediately charted on the child's progress notes. Charts were used to compare the clients' behaviors over the four weeks period. The charted client data was then compared to see if there was any progression in positive behavior. Some behaviors were not observed, for example, a child may have come to the staff saying that a peer hit him, or cursed at him. The behaviors noted were only those that were observed, and could be recognized, by the staff.

Results

The data were analyzed using frequencies, correlations, standard deviations, and means. Due to the extremely low level of occurrence of homicidal ideations and sexual acting out, these categories were excluded from the analysis. In Table 1 the primary behavioral manifestations are listed along with the mean and standard deviation.

Table 1

Behavioral Manifestations

	N	Minimum	Maximum	Sum	Mean	Std. Deviation
AGE	5	7.00	10.00	42.00	8.4000	1.34164
Oppositional/ Defiance	5	234.00	404.00	1434.00	286.8000	69.12814
Interventions	5	5.00	13.00	45.00	9.0000	3.08221
Physical Aggression	5	35.00	57.00	225.00	45.0000	9.40744
Verbal Outbursts	5	41.00	125.00	338.00	67.6000	33.56784
Valid N (listwise)	5					

The hypothesis focused on explored whether or not the therapeutic environment helped the young BPD clients get treatment or held them back. A question that can be asked is whether or not it is beneficial to group similarly aged children with very similar diagnoses. It is apparent that mania can be triggered by a client being in an over-stimulating environment, and because children with BPD cycle so quickly, being grouped with similarly diagnosed children may cause an increase in negative behavior. It was observed early in the study that Client M appeared to be the primary aggressor (Table 2). He was much bigger than the other children and showed more aggression.

Table 2
Weekly Acts of Physical Aggression

NAME				WEEK1	WEEK2	WEEK3	WEEK4
NAME	Client A	1		14.00	13.00	20.00	10.00
		Total	N	1	1	1	1
	Client B	1		13.00	10.00	14.00	10.00
		Total	N	1	1	1	1
	Client J	1		7.00	6.00	13.00	10.00
		Total	N	1	1	1	1
	Client M	1		22.00(b)	14.00(b)	13.00	1.00
		Total	N	1	1	1	1
	Client W	1		8.00	7.00	11.00	10.00
		Total	N	1	1	1	1
	Total	N		5	5	5	5
*Client M's physical aggression is higher than his peers							

The empirical evidence showed that there was a significant trend in week 3. 80% of the clients, excluding Client M, had an increase in oppositional behavior and physical aggressiveness. They also required more interventions that week. Figure 1 shows the change in these behavioral manifestations for week 3. The mean number of incidents per person (physical aggression, oppositional behavior, and interventions) over the whole study is compared to the mean number of incidents for just week three.

Figure 1

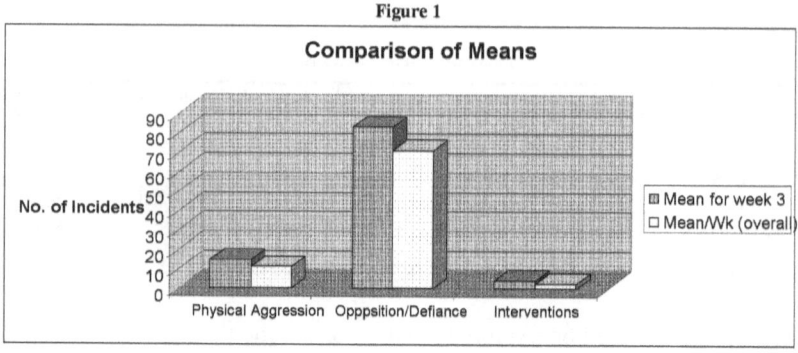

Client M was moved from the primary in a therapeutic attempt to decrease his aggressiveness towards peers. He was moved in week 2 and his physical aggression decreased from 14 incidents in week 2, to 13 incidents in week 3, then again down to 1 incident in week 4 (Figure 2). His verbal outbursts decreased 86% in week 3; his oppositional behavior decreased 31%, and he required no interventions throughout the study. While Client M was showing a great improvement it is also noted that one external variable not listed is the fact that Client M was now the youngest and smallest child in his new living area. On the other hand, the children surrounding Client M were all on the highest levels so there may have been some positive influence by those around him.

Figure 2

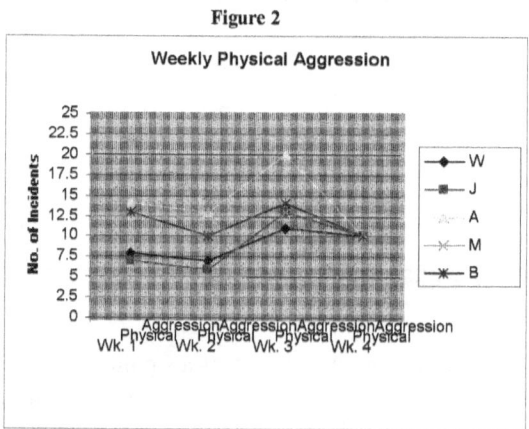

Only Client J had a significant change in his medications. No trend, in terms of medication, was found among the others. His therapy indicated in week 3 that physical holds were too traumatic for him. The recommendation was to allow him to listen to music in the timeout room, when he was agitated, which became the coping skill that was promoted. The changes noted were his decrease in interventions (75%), his verbal outbursts (42%), and oppositional behavior (12%).

Figure 3

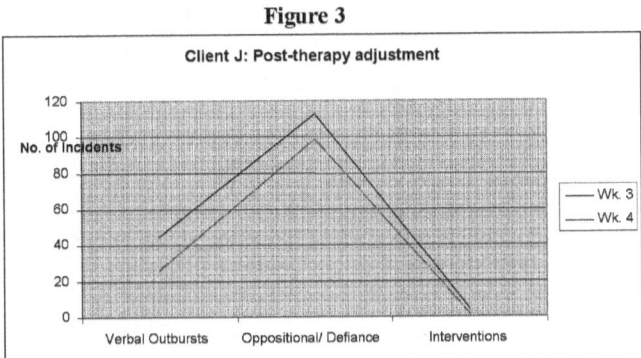

In reference to Figure 3, the strongest positive correlation was between oppositional behavior and verbal outbursts. Physical aggression and verbal outbursts had the most negative correlation. It appeared that most of the time when a child became extremely agitated, he became non-verbal, and would only act out his anger. This was referred to as a coping skill by one resident (destroying property). Client B stated, "I just want to hit him and then I feel better again." They were usually able to calm down on their own after exerting so much energy. It was the times that they were oppositional and defiant that required so much effort and led to interventions. Some examples were running around the unit, jumping on the furniture, and being disruptive and unsafe.

Table 3
Correlations of Interventions
with
Physical Aggressiion, Outbursts, and Defiance

		Physical Aggression	Verbal Outbursts	Oppositional/ Defiance	Interventions
Physical Aggression	Pearson Correlation	1	-.645	-.479	-.526
	Sig. (1-tailed)	.	.120	.207	.181
Verbal Outbursts	Pearson Correlation	-.645	1	.868(*)	.546
	Sig. (1-tailed)	.120	.	.028	.170
Oppositional/ Defiance	Pearson Correlation	-.479	.868(*)	1	.630
	Sig. (1-tailed)	.207	.028	.	.127
Interventions	Pearson Correlation	-.526	.546	.630	1
	Sig. (1-tailed)	.181	.170	.127	.

*Correlation is significant

This supported the hypothesis that the environment did affect the person and his behavior. On the other hand, the other residents had an increase in behavioral manifestations. It is uncertain that the other children's behavioral changes were related to the loss of the aggressor, Client M, but there seemed to be an association. In addition to a more comfortable environment, the children were able to socialize a lot more easily and without the fear that a peer would create physical chaos. They seemed to hold group a lot more easily and completed it. It was observed that even when mood changes occurred, coping skills were immediately implemented. Client W stated, "Can I take a self timeout because I am getting frustrated?" Client J was able to remain in his designated area when he was agitated. He excused himself and closed the door to his room. He turned on his radio and would lie down while usually throwing paper airplanes around his room. The others showed very little change, but as was witnessed the changing environment can affect the child in a positive way. These children with BPD and other mood disorders were showing great effort to manage behaviors. It was easier for them to control mania induced episodes by implementing coping strategies, talking to their staff, and using positive peer contact.

Most of the observed incidents were present in the early part of the shift (3 p.m. to 5:30 p.m.). Usually after dinner, at 5:30 p. m., the children were full, and were generally relaxed in their rooms while they prepared for showers and dorm jobs. After a few of the children's hygiene requirements, the meds were administered at 6 p.m. The observations showed that about thirty minutes to an hour and a half after the administration, the children became lethargic and too unmotivated to cause trouble.

The use of continuity of care with schedule adherence along with very strict and consistent day to day operations was the most beneficial in their treatment. This researcher/ observer would propose that the treatment team not put too many of the same diagnosed children together, just to avoid a domino effect.

Discussion

The articles reviewed indicated that the overall diagnoses of BPD in adolescents and children are rising. The knowledge of heritability in bipolar clients has given science a heads up on the potential outcome of the children and adolescents of adults who have the disease. Previously children were misdiagnosed, primarily, with either depression or ADHD, which resulted in improper treatment procedures. Children using the wrong medication have shown an increase in manic episodes and more drastic lows including MD disorders.

Since there is now knowledge of genetics and their effect on kids, the opportunity to catch and treat these symptoms and provide earlier therapeutic and medical interventions is available. If these symptoms go untreated there may be further co-morbidity and uncontrollable behaviors leading to failure in school, lack of social interaction, overly impulsive behavior, and hospitalization.

The behaviors noticed in this research were aligned with those in the reviewed studies. The children exhibited aggressive attitudes, restlessness, were easily agitated, had impulse control problems, and were emotionally unstable. After proper medication changes within the residential treatment center, the behaviors somewhat subsided. The conclusions are that the offspring of BPD clients should become more aware of the high potential that their children will be affected by this disease, and that earlier diagnosis is critical. It is also crucial that early intervention take place to avoid further downfall by the child which could consequently create a highly unstable and uncontrollable adult. The findings from this research support that environmental interventions can help to stabilize symptoms in these children.

There must always be flexibility among those who are exposed to these children, and an open mind to help them with their therapy. It is the opinion of this researcher/observer, that the child must have a role model and the motivation to learn to change his behavior. Once the habit is formed in managing manic, or hypo-manic episodes, the child may resume life in society and feel more comfortable with himself.

References

Caramagno, Thomas C (1998). Manic-depressive psychosis and critical approaches to Virginia Woolf's life and work. *PMLA, Vol. 103, No. 1.* pp. 10-23.

Fitzgerald, Bill (2006). An existential view of adolescent development. *Adolescence, Vol. 40, No. 160,* pp. 174-179.

Gibson, Donna M. & Jefferson, Renee N. (2006). The effect of the perceived parental involvement and the use of growth fostering relationships on the self concept in adolescents participating in Gear Up, *Adolescence, Vol. 41, No. 161,* pp. 113-125.

Krout, Maurice (1938). A note on Dunham's contribution to the ecology of functional psychoses. *American Sociological Review, Vol. 3, No. 2,* pp. 209-212.

Mestas, Miranda. & Urdan, Tim. (2006). The Goals behind setting goals. *Journal of Educational Psychology, Vol. 98, No. 2,* pp. 354-365.

Patel, Nick C, Delbello, Melissa P, & Strakowski, Stephen M. (2006). Ethnic differences in symptom presentation of youths with bipolar disorder. *Bipolar Disorders, Vol.8,* pp. 95-99.

Rabinowitz, Daniel & Yang, Qiong (1999). Testing for age-at-onset anticipation with affected parent-child pairs. *Biometrics, Vol. 55, No. 3,* pp. 834-838.

Shink, E., Morissette, J., Sherrington, R. & Barden, N. (2005). A Genome-wide scan points to a susceptibility locus for bipolar disorder on chromosome 12. *Molecular Psychiatry, 10,* pp. 545-552.

Tomb M.D. & David A. *Psychiatry, DSM IV: Fifth Edition,* 1995 Williams, Wilkins, Baltimore, MD

Adolescent Deviance: Human Development and Social Forces

Logan Blackmon
Junior, Psychology Major

(Dr. Debra L. Murphy, Major Advisor for Psychology)

Abstract

Crimes are disproportionately committed by adolescents and young adults in America. Nearly 10% of America's youth aged 12-17 are introduced to the juvenile justice system yearly. With the purpose of explaining why this trend continues, case analysis was conducted with two adolescent boys. Responses were extracted from a discussion with two clients who represented extreme ends of the developmental spectrum. The discussion focused on criminal behavior and misconduct in schools. Their answers were examined within the context of psychological, social and moral development that the literature has indicated is reflective of adolescents. Through content analysis, the responses were compared and categorized in terms of their consistency with the theoretical perspectives of Erickson, Kohlberg and Social Learning Theory (Weiten, 2008). The results of the research suggested why crimes are disproportionately committed by adolescents and what could potentially decrease these rates.

Literature Review

In an effort to discover the relationship between crime rates and adolescents, sociological and psychological theories were examined. A review of scientific studies, research articles and data served as a basis for generating this paper and exploring the factors associated with adolescent crime rates. Demographics extracted from the Juvenile Court Statistics Data Book (Puzzanchera and Kang (2007) were used to demonstrate baseline crime rates. It reported that crime rates peaked between the ages of 13 and 15, and descended with age. Theoretical perspectives in psychology support this data, offering expected behavioral patterns within various age groups. The review of literature on Kohlberg's Stages of Moral Development, Erickson's Stages of Social Development, and Social Learning Theory shed light on stages within each where there may be vulnerability to delinquency that can explain the higher tendency toward crime rates at certain ages (Weiten, 2008).

The social developmental model of Erick Erickson was a focus in this study's examination of the variables associated with criminality among adolescents. Ages thirteen through fifteen, noted as the ages when most crimes occur, are also referred to by Erickson as the peak of adolescence. Adolescence is a transitional period from childhood to adulthood, often referred to as a second birth. According to Haynie (2001).

The expectations of what will result after carrying out a behavior combined with whether the individual values the outcome of the behavior determines if the behavior will occur. For example, if a child is rewarded with money for good grades on their report card, money reinforces the continuation of making good grades if the child values money. However, if the child does not value money, it will not serve to reinforce. Centered upon learning from others, the social learning theory is deeply entwined with the adolescent stage of development. Throughout adolescence, individuals adopt the habits of social learning, observing their peers, parents, media images and other formal institutions. By observing others, a basis of what rewards in life come with what identities is discovered. Consequently the models with the most perks, such as popularity and monetary items, are integrated into identities. Adolescents pressure their peers to make behavioral choices that might otherwise be rejected, because the desire to be liked and to be apart of the group is so strong at this stage, plus curiosity is often a contributing force (Lohman, 1959).

During identity development, delinquents with positive feelings toward and close attachments to controlling institutions and persons, such as, school officials and family, in authority over the decision making process are far more likely to develop identifies that are resilient to criminality. Haynie (2001) found the following. "The presence of authority that was *psychological* rather than *physical* was more of a deterrent, due to the thought of consequences." An association of adolescents with family, school and church, lessened criminal behavior, because of their role in molding attitudes and behavior in a positive and productive manner. Criminal activity increases during after school hour and the summer months, if there are not recreational alternatives for adolescents, suggesting an association of delinquency with the absence of structure and authoritative figures. Jang and Thornberry (1998) make the following point. "These alternatives can help to prepare the child to face life challenges effectively and transition from familial dependence to self reliance with less confusion, which can contribute to his success."

Past research suggests that adolescents' inquisitive characteristics and need for acceptance and immature thinking patterns place them at risk for misconduct and criminal behavior. The high reports of crimes and misconduct may also be due to differences in misconduct definitions between adults and adolescents. For example, what adults consider as criminal misconduct may not be viewed as so by adolescents. Recidivism rates and age demographics in crime reports support this data. As a teen matures, gains responsibility and their thinking patterns become more mature, their definitions of criminal behavior become consistent with that of adults and they are less likely to commit crimes.

Kohlberg's Stages of Moral Development holds that moral reasoning, the basis for ethical behavior, is developed through experience that stimulates ethical mental processes. Lerner (1999) makes the following point. "Individuals discuss and debate with others, and views are questioned and challenged resulting in analyses of wrong and right which stimulates moral reasoning." During stage one of Kohlberg's theory the focus is on the direct consequences that actions have on the individual self. Morality is based on the level of punishment for an act, so that the worse the punishment, the worse the act is perceived to be. What is in the best interest to self and need satisfaction determine morality in stage two. Individuals begin conformity to the majority culture during the third stage. Right and wrong is determined by close others' approval or disapproval. Individuals begin considering intentions and reciprocity

Societal rules and laws determine morality in the fourth stage (Lerner, 1999). As individuals transcend from one stage to the next when they progress through life experiences, an increase in cognitive capacity levels occurs.

Adolescence is a transitional phase of development between childhood and adulthood. They are susceptible to crime due to the absence of firm morals and a societal perspective. Adolescents are egocentric and vulnerable to acceptance by their peers as they are struggling with identity formation. Adolescents will be less likely to participate in deviant behavior if they interact with positive role models and societal ideals and customs offering constructive activities, as well as, individuals who assist youth during times of developmental confusion and identity formation. Behavioral expectations must be adjusted to fit the maturity levels of adolescents. This is a plausible hypothesis, particularly in light of our increasing knowledge of how developmental phases during adolescence greatly influence judgment call and behavior.

Methods

The case study method was used. The individuals who participated in the study included a fourteen year old male who was active in a gang and had been introduced to the criminal justice system. Another fourteen year old male focused on during the discussion exemplified respect, responsibility and great decision making. The two participants were selected to represent both ends of the spectrum. As a means of understanding the developmental stage of moral cognitive patterns of individuals at ages 12-16 with regard to crime and misconduct in school, a set of questions was designed and used to generate a discussion within a group of adolescents. The focus was to better understand these adolescent's emergent developmental perspectives on crime and deviant behavior. The intent was to identify the thinking patterns that lead an adolescent to criminal activity, identify their moral standing and source, and analyze what is viewed as justification for police/authoritative intervention. The data for this study were gathered by qualitative analyses of reflections pertaining to the answers, which included hypothetical reactions to the questions listed below.

- What is a crime?
- What should definitely get a person picked up by the cops?
- How do you feel about gang activity?
- Why do people join gangs?
- How do you feel about teens writing on public property
  o How should it be handled by law enforcement?
- Once you think about breaking the law or participating in misbehavior,

what usually stops you?

- Why do you do things that you know are wrong?
- Is it ever OK to commit a crime?
  o When and why?
- What do you think about talking back in schools and to parents?
  o What should be the consequences other than calling the cops or getting sent to another school?
- If a child is running through the hall and slaps the bottom of the opposite sex, is this a crime or misbehavior
- When you get in trouble at school for things like slapping a girl's bottom, cursing a teacher, or fighting, is it explained why certain behaviors are inappropriate or is there any conversation before or after you get in trouble?
- How do you feel about school?
  o Is it a waste of time?
  o Is it benefiting you?
- What do you do after school hours?

Analysis

Each question listed above was woven into the discussion and the adolescents' responses were analyzed qualitatively by gleaning from the responses why they participated in behaviors that are unlawful or against school codes. Using content analysis, the responses were compared and contrasted and categorized in terms of consistency with the theoretical perspectives of Erickson, Kohlberg, and Social Learning Theory.

Results

Listed below are the responses extracted from the discussion with two adolescent boys. The discussion focused on what constitutes a crime, and what provokes an adolescent to commit a crime.

- What is a crime?

Respondent A: *Anything the cops can pick you up for. If nobody can't call the cops on you for it then it ain't no crime.*

Respondent B: *Something that a person does that is against the law, like stealing or killing somebody.*

- What should definitely get a person picked up by the cops?

Respondent A: *Killing somebody, jacking cars and people.*

Respondent B: *Killing somebody, robbing somebody.*

- How do you feel about gang activity? Why do people join gangs?

Respondent A: *It's cool. Them are you fam. The cops will pick you up for it though. People join gangs 'cause your friends are in it and if they your friends anyway then why not join? They always got your back. They like your brothers and sisters. It's crunk.*

Respondent B: *Some of them are cool. Some of the people are cool and some are not. They get in trouble at school a lot and get picked up by the cops, but they not all bad. They in gangs 'cause of friends or like family or something like if they cousin or something is in it, like for different reasons. Like he said some people just do it just because. Because other people do it, they copy off somebody else.*

- How do you feel about teens

writing on public property? How should it be handled by law enforcement?

Respondent A: *They be trying to lock up my peoples and give tickets and stuff but people gone clean it off and stuff anyway. I know people get paid for it. People just doing they job. They getting paid to do they job, so why they complaining?*

Respondent B: *It ain't no big deal but sometimes people be writing all on people stuff. That ain't right. But like he said, people do be getting paid to just cover it up so why is it a big deal?*

• Once you think about breaking the law or participating in misbehavior, what usually stops you?

Respondent A: *Like if I know I'm gone get caught, somebody gone call the cops. If it's my last chance or something, sometimes it ain't worth it. You just got to chill sometimes.*

Respondent B: *If I know I'm gone get caught, then I'm not gone do it. And some stuff is just wrong, like killing somebody and stealing. Like I know people who like steal from other people...like video games and like shoes and money. And I don't want nobody taking nothing from me. My momma said what goes around comes around and it's true 'cause it happened to me before.*

• Why do you do things that you know are wrong?

Respondent A: *I don't know. I don't really be thinking about if it's wrong or not. I just do it. It's fun. Like with your friends and stuff, we just are having fun. We be like, let's do it, and then we do it. And then we be like dang if we get caught and if we don't, then that's what's up.*

Respondent B: *Man what goes around comes around, like bad stuff that I don't want nobody to do to me then I ain't gone do it but like if we just having fun then it's cool. Like curfew and stuff, that's some _____ (expletive). Like stuff like n_____ (the "n" word) knocking (knocking on doors and running away before an answer), curfew, and like when we be fighting and stuff, we ain't hurting nobody so it ain't nothing. But I ain't down with like killing people and stealing and stuff. That ain't cool.*

• Is it ever OK to commit a crime? When and why?

Respondent A: *It ain't like OK, but like if you ain't gone get caught then it ain't no big deal. And like if like you stealing or something and you know they got more or they can get more then it ain't hurting nothing. Or like if somebody do something to you, then you have to do it back. Like if somebody like disrespecting you, then you got to do it back.*

Respondent B: *I think it's OK like if it's self defense, like if somebody is trying to hurt you or your family. Other than that, it ain't OK, but like if you not really hurting nobody doing it like stealing a candy or something from a store then it ain't no big deal 'cause you not hurting nobody.*

• What do you think about talking back in schools and to parents? What should be the consequences? (versus calling the cops or getting sent to another school)

Respondent A: *Man sometimes you just be like_____ (expletive) it. You just don't feel like being bothered and they want to bother you. Like in class,* the teachers and stuff be wanting to get cussed out. They just be taunting you. Just get out my face and leave me alone. And they be real disrespectful too. They want to talk to you like they your moms or something, and call you out in front of people. They be doing that on purpose. That ____(expletive) ain't cool. And then when you say something they be all embarrassed and mad and want to suspend you, saying we don't know who the adults are, but whatever, respect me. Ain't nobody 'bout to talk to me crazy. My momma don't even do that.

Respondent B: *Them teachers do be tripping a lot. It's like if you don't feel like being bothered, then that's when they wanna be all up in your face and stuff. That ain't cool. Like this one dude, like he had a fight with the teacher at school 'cause the dude was all in his face and stuff 'cause he had his head down on the desk. And dude fams had got picked up by immigration the day before, so he was just like on chill all day. So the teacher like got all up in his face and was talking all loud in front of everybody and so homey got up and got in his face right back, and then just hit him and they start fighting. It never would have happened if he would have just let homey chill for a minute. Teachers be thinking that they your parents and stuff and can talk to you any kind of way. That ain't right 'cause if you talk to them like that they gone try to send you down and stuff, but like that's the same thing with us. We don't want you all in our face either. Respect goes both ways. And it don't even be necessary to like call the cops and get people kicked out of school and*

stuff. Sometime you just got to chill out for a minute.

- If a child is running through the hall and slaps the bottom of the opposite sex, is this a crime or misbehavior?

Respondent A: *It ain't like nobody having sex or something, we be just playing around. They be making a big deal out of nothing, and most of the time the girls don't even be tripping. It be the teachers. They just be trying to get people in trouble for nothing just because they don't like you. It's not a crime 'cause the cops don't care if you touching some _____(slang for buttocks). It's just the teachers that be tripping. That's they rules, not the cops.*

Respondent B: *I don't even think it is misbehavior but it do break that rule about keeping your hands to yourself. But it ain't no crime at all. Can't nobody put you in jail for that. Teachers be trying make it a big deal and stuff, but you be really just playing around, kind of like tag, but you just touching a little _____(slang for buttocks) or something. And like he said the girls don't be tripping and I sure ain't gone trip if a girl does it to me. It's nothing.*

- When you get in trouble at school for things like slapping a girls bottom, cursing a teacher, and fighting, is it explained why certain behaviors are inappropriate or is there any conversation before or after you get in trouble?

Respondent A: *They don't be trying to have no conversation with us... they just be like you want to get kicked* out...it could be for a good reason or something and they not even trying to hear it. You get your referral and go to the office, and then you sit in "In School Suspension" all day and can't say nothing all day. Or you just get suspended and you got to sit in the office until they talk to like your moms or somebody and then they send you home. Sometimes they even call the cops.

Respondent B: *Nope they really don't be trying to talk to nobody. Once you in trouble it's like you don't have no rights. If you be like trying to explain then they will suspend you talking 'bout you disturbing the piece or some mess like that. They always take the teacher's side for anything too. The teacher could be wrong and the people in the office won't even listen.*

- How do you feel about school? Is it a waste of time...is it benefiting you?

Respondent A: *Man it's fun sometimes 'cause you can like kick it with all of your friends but sometimes the teachers be tripping... All that stuff they be talking 'bout in school, we not gone need that. My brother told me that. I'm gone get my GED. My brother got a good job getting paid and he quit school, got a GED and he getting paid. I just go because I can't drive or get a job but when I turn 16 I'm gone get my GED and get a job because I'm all about my dough, about this paper. Ya'll gone be still running around with your lunch money and I'm gone be paid.*

Respondent B: *It is but it's boring and the teachers be getting on your nerves too much. Like if you want to get a good job and stuff you gotta' go to school*

and learn because don't nobody want to hire no dummy but for real some of this school stuff is wack. I think the teachers retarded for real though. They be tripping on some of them rules...I got in trouble at lunch for wrestling, talking 'bout we was fighting, that was my patna, we wasn't even fighting. Dumb!

- What do you do after school hours?

Respondent A: *Man, go to like HEB, fill up carts and leave. Go to McDonalds. Everybody be up there. Come to the learning center, depending on who here or what's going on, or just go home and play the game or something.*

Respondent B: *I play the game with my friend or come to the learning center.*

Discussion

The analyses of the participants' perceptions pertaining to deviance are associated with the Kohlberg, Erickson and Social Learning Theory perspectives. Erickson's explanation of adolescence as a period when individuals are reliant upon the acceptance of others, are struggling to develop an identity and are experiencing an increase in emotions is reflected in their responses.

Kohlberg's four stages of moral development describe adolescents' moral reasoning and views of society. In the first stage, obedience and punishment orientation, individual reasoning behavior is based on the level of punishment directly associated with a behavior. During stage two an individual deciphers right and wrong egocentrically by what is in the individual's best interest. In the third stage right and wrong is determined by close other's approval or disapproval, as well as, intentions and reciprocity. Authority and society's rules and laws are the determining factors during the fourth stage.

Social Learning Theory illustrates how adolescents' behaviors and identities are based on values and expectations of rewards if certain behaviors occur. The following equation was used in evaluating the respondents' behavior: Behavioral Potential= Expectations + Value. The likelihood of an individual carrying out a behavior is determined by an expected outcome of the behavior in conjunction with whether or not the individual values the outcome which will then reinforce the behavior. Below the responses are interpreted within the context of each stage.

Relation of Adolescents' Responses to Developmental Theories

Kohlberg's Theoretical Perspective

Q: What is crime?

(A) *Anything the cops can pick you up for. If nobody can't call the cops on you for it then it ain't no crime.*

Kohlberg's Stage 1: Crime is defined based on level of punishment and cop involvement.

Q: How do you feel about teens writing on public property? How should it be handled by law enforcement?

(A) *They be trying to lock up my peoples and give tickets and stuff but people gon' clean it off and stuff anyway. They getting paid to do they job, so why they complaining?*

(B) *It ain't no big deal but sometimes people be writing all on people stuff. That ain't right.*

Kohlberg's Stage 2: The feelings of others are not considered, which exemplifies egocentrism. Social ordinance is not understood. That some are paid to clean graffiti is more important to them than the principle of the matter.

Q: Once you think about breaking the law or participating in misbehavior, what usually stops you?

(B) *If I know I'm gon' get caught, then I'm not gon' do it. And some stuff is just wrong, like killing somebody and stealing. And I don't want nobody taking nothing from me. My momma said what goes around comes around and it's true 'cause it happened to me before.*

Kohlberg's Stage 3: He doesn't want to make anyone feel the way that he has felt before, and considers doing the right thing.

Q: Why do you do things that you know are wrong?

(A) *I don't know. I don't really be thinking about if it's wrong or not. I just do it. It's fun.*

(B) *Man what goes around comes around, like bad stuff that I don't want nobody to do to me then I ain't gon' do it but like if we just having fun then it's cool. Like curfew and stuff, that's some _____ (expletive). Like stuff like _____ (the "n" word) knocking (knocking on doors and running away before an answer), curfew, and like when we be fighting and stuff, we ain't hurting nobody so it ain't nothing. But I ain't down with like killing people and stealing and stuff. That ain't cool.*

Relation to Kohlberg's Stage 1: Respondent A participates based on consequences.

Relation to Kohlberg's Stage 3: Respondent B knows he is breaking the law, but he considers others' intentions and does not purposefully hurt others.

Q: Is it ever OK to commit a crime?

(A) *It ain't like OK, but like if you ain't gon' get caught then it ain't no big deal. And like if like you stealing or something and you know they got more or they can get more then it ain't hurting nothing. Or like if somebody do something to you, then you have to do it back.*

Kohlberg's Stage 4: The respondent lacks a perspective of social ordinance. They feel justified .if they can get more.

Kohlberg's Stage 3: They feel that their behavior is justified because no one is believed to be severely affected.

Kohlberg's Stage 1: It's OK if you will not get caught. The crime is downplayed.

Q: If a child is running through the hall and slaps the bottom of the opposite sex, is this a crime or misbehavior?

(A) *It ain't like nobody having sex or something, we be just playing around. They be making a big deal out of nothing, and most of the time the girls don't even be tripping. It be the teachers. It's not a crime 'cause the cops don't care if you touching some _____ (slang for buttocks).*

Kohlberg's Stage 1: It is not viewed as a problem because of the few consequences.

Q: How do you feel about school? Is it a waste of time? Is it benefiting you?

(B) *It is but it's boring and the teachers be getting on your nerves too much. Like if you wanna' get a good job and stuff, you gotta' go to school and learn because don't nobody want*

to hire no dummy, but for real some of this school stuff is wack.

Kohlberg's Stage 2: The respondent believes in the rewards of going to school.

Q: What do you think about talking back in schools and to parents? What should be the consequences?

(A) *Man sometimes you just be like _____ (expletive) it. You just don't feel like being bothered and they want to bother you. Like in class, the teachers and stuff be wanting to get cussed out. They just be taunting you. Just get out my face and leave me alone. And they be real disrespectful too. They want to talk to you like they your moms or something, and call you out in front of people. That _____ (expletive) ain't cool. And then when you say something they be all embarrassed and mad and want to suspend you, saying we don't know who the adults are, but whatever, respect me.*

(B) *And dude fams had got picked up by immigration the day before, so he was just like on chill all day. So the teacher like got all up in his face and was talking all loud in front of everybody and so homey got up and got in his face right back, and then just hit him and they start fighting. It never would have happened if he would have just let homey chill for a minute. Teachers be thinking that they your parents and stuff and can talk to you any kind of way. That ain't right 'cause if you talk to them like that they gon' try to send you down and stuff, but like that's the same thing with us. We don't want you all in our face either. Respect goes both ways.*

Kohlberg's Stage 4: They are considering the intentions of both parties. They believe that teachers disrespect and taunt students intentionally. Therefore, cursing a teacher is justified.

Social Learning Theory (SLT)

Q: How do you feel about gang activity? Why do people join gangs?

(A) *The cops will pick you up for it though. People join gangs 'cause your friends are in it and if they your friends anyway then why not join? They always got your back. They like your brothers and sisters. It's crunk.*

(B) *They in gangs 'cause of friends or like family or something like if they cousin or something is in it, like for different reasons. Like he said some people just do it just because. Because other people do it, they copy off somebody else.*

SLT: When close family and friends are affiliated, behaviors are learned quickly. Some of the rewards that potentially accompany gang affiliation is spending more time with friends and family, popularity, protection from others, and gaining friendship.

Q: If a child is running through the hall and slaps the bottom of the opposite sex, is this a crime or misbehavior?

(B) *I don't even think it is misbehavior but it do break that rule about keeping your hands to yourself. But it ain't no crime at all. Can't nobody put you in jail for that. Teachers be trying to make it a big deal and stuff, but you be really just playing around, kind of like tag, but you just touching a little _____ (slang for buttocks) or something. And like he said the girls don't be tripping and I sure ain't gon' trip if a girl does that to me. It's nothing.*

SLT: They learn through the media that attention from a guy to a girl may bring monetary items to the girl and make him feel more masculine.

Q: How do you feel about school? Is it a waste of time? Is it benefiting you?

(A) *Man it's fun sometimes 'cause you can like kick it with all of your friends but sometimes the teachers be tripping. All that stuff they be talking 'bout in school, we not gon' need that. My brother told me that. I'm gon' get my GED. My brother got a good job getting paid and he quit school, got a GED and he getting paid.*

SLT: He has chosen to take the same route as his brother stemming from observing the rewards of having money, respect, and girls, which is envied.

Q: What do you think about talking back in schools and to parents? What should be the consequences?

(A) *Man sometimes you just be like _____ (expletive) it. You just don't feel like being bothered and they want to bother you. Like in class, the teachers and stuff be wanting to get cussed out. They just be taunting you. Just get out my face and leave me alone. And they be real disrespectful too.*

(B) *And dude fams had got picked up by immigration the day before, so he was just like on chill all day. So the teacher like got all up in his face and was talking all loud in front of everybody and so homey got up and got in his face right back, and then just hit him and they start fighting.*

SLT: They have observed that violence alleviates problems which they emulate.

Erikson's Developmental Model

Q: How do you feel about gang activity? Why do people join gangs?

(A) *It's cool. Them are you fam. They always got your back. They like your brothers and sisters. It's crunk.*

(B) *Some of them are cool. Some of the people are cool and some are not. They get in trouble at school a lot and get picked up by the cops, but they not all bad.*

Erickson: Gang affiliation offers many friends and the acceptance and respect of peers outside the gang. If friends are already apart of a gang it is likely that you will join in order to remain a member of the peer group.

Q: Why do you do things that you know are wrong?

(A) *I don't know. I don't really be thinking about if it's wrong or not. I just do it. It's fun. Like with your friends and stuff, we just are having fun. We be like, let's do it, and then we do it.*

Erickson: Adolescents act on impulse which is what the response exemplifies.

Q: Is it ever OK to commit a crime? When and why?

(B) *It ain't like OK, but like if you ain't gon' get caught then it ain't no big deal. And like if like you stealing or something and you know they got more or they can get more then it ain't hurting nothing. Or like if somebody do something to you, then you have to do it back.*

Erickson: This respondent's ideals of justification for committing a crime are not developed. He debates over whether defense is the only justification or if it would be OK if no one was hurt from crime.

Q: What do you think about talking back in schools and to parents? What should be the consequences?

(A) *Man sometimes you just be like _____ (expletive) it. You just don't feel* like being bothered and they want to bother you. Like in class, the teachers and stuff be wanting to get cussed out. They just be taunting you. Just get out my face and leave me alone. And they be real disrespectful too. They want to talk to you like they your moms or something, and call you out in front of people.*

(B) *Dude fams had got picked up by immigration, so he was just like on chill all day. So the teacher like got all up in his face and was talking all loud in front of everybody and so homey got up and got in his face right back and then just hit him and they start fighting.*

Erickson: The respondents are experiencing emotions that they are having difficulty expressing and dealing with. Grief, frustration, sympathy, etc. become more complex as one develops. When teachers confront students in front of peers and speak to them in a ways in which may be viewed as disrespectful, the student typically retaliates because of what peers may think if they do not.

Q: What do you do after school hours?

(A) *Man, go to like HEB, fill up carts and leave. Go to McDonalds. Everybody be up there. Come to the learning center, depending on who here or what's going on, or just go home and play the game or something.*

Erickson: The respondent acts on impulse and follows the behaviors of his peer group in order to remain apart of the peer group.

Through content analysis, it was discovered that criminal activity peaks during adolescence due to the immaturity of morals and identity, which provides a venue for peers to have greater influence on one another. Level of reasoning also proved to be a significant factor as well, when determining why teens act out. The data collected supported an association between adolescence, when crime rates peak, and developmental stage characteristics that may make teens vulnerable to delinquency. During the years of adolescence, there is a need for positive role models, structured activity, and outlets for teens to discuss their feelings and thoughts. As an adolescent, teens are egocentric and are looking to do things that are the most satisfying to them without thinking of others' feelings or consequences. As well, teens typically participate in misconduct simply because they want to or to alleviate boredom. As an individual's exposure and experience grows in society, so does maturity. It was concluded that if teens can gain greater exposure to formal institutions, if behavioral expectations can be adjusted to meet levels of maturation, and they can be encouraged to cultivate desirable morals and ideals, they will be less likely to succumb to juvenile delinquency and experience a proper transition to adulthood.

References

Dornbusch, S. M. (1989). The Sociology of Adolescence. *Annual Review of Sociology.15*, 233-259.

Furstenberg, F. F. (November 2000). The Sociology of Adolescence and Youth in the 1990's: A Critical Commentary. *Journal of Marriage and Family. 62*(4), 896-910.

Giordano, P., Groat, T., Pugh, M. D. & Swinfor, S. P. (March 1998). The Quality of Adolescent Friendships: Long Term Effects? *Journal of Health and Social Behavior. 39*(1), 55-71.

Haynie, D. L. (January 2001). Delinquent Peers Revisited: Does Network Structure Matter? *The American Journal of Sociology. 106* (106), 1013-1057.

Jang, S. J. & Thornberry, T. P. (August 1998). Self-Esteem, Delinquent Peers, and Delinquency: A Test of the Self-Enhancement Thesis. *American Sociological Review. 63*(4), 586-598.

Lerner, R. (1999). Cognitive and Moral Development, Academic Achievement in Adolescence. New York, NY: Routledge

Lohman, J. D. (1959). Juvenile Delinquency: A Social Dimensiion. *The Journal of Negro Education. 28*(3), 286-299.

Monahan, T. P. (December 1961). On the Trend in Delinquency. *Social Forces. 40*(2), 158-168.

Puzzanchera, K. & Kang, W. (2007, November 12). Juvenile Court Statistics Databook: Demographic Characteristics. *Juvenile Courts Statistic Data Book.* Retrieved October 10, 2007, from http://ojjdp.ncjrc.gov/ojststbb/jcsdb/

Reckless, W. C. (April 1937). Juvenile Delinquency and Behavior Patterning. *Journal of Educational Sociology. 10*(8), 493-505.

Weiten, W. *Psychology Themes and Variations: Briefer Version,* (7th Edition), Las Vegas, Nevada. Thomson-Wadsworth, 2008, 304-337.

Zorbaugh, H. L. & Payne, V. L. (February 1935). Adolescence: Psychosis or Social Adjustment. *Journal of Educational Sociology. 8* (6), 371-377.

Effects of Abuse Among Adolescent Women*

Soleil Hernandez
Senior, Psychology Major

Jane Dimmitt Champion, Ph.D., F.N.P., C.N.S., F.A.A.N., Principal
Investigator & Professor and
Director, Center for Community-Based Health Promotion for
Women and Children-University of Texas Health Science Center at
San Antonio
(Summer Internship Advisor)

Supported by a Grant (1 R01 DA019180-01) From the National
Institute on Drug Abuse

*Article is based on a secondary data analysis of Dr. Dimmit
Champion's study at the University of Texas Medical School at
San Antonio when Soleil Hernandez was a
NIDA Summer Intern (2008)

(Dr. Debra L. Murphy, Major Advisor for Psychology)

Abstract

This study is a secondary analysis of a subset of Dr. Dimmit Champion's data from an ongoing controlled-randomized trial of African- and Mexican-American adolescent females who have a history of sexually transmitted infection (STI) and/or abuse. This analysis was conducted to explore the association of sexual risk behavior, substance use, and psychosocial elements of depression and sexual ownership among the participants. The analysis consisted of African-and Mexican-American adolescent women aged 13-19 years (n = 250) with sexually transmitted infection (STI) and a history of physical, sexual or psychological abuse. Participants completed a semi-structured interview regarding their health-seeking behaviors, perceptions of self-worth, sexual health history, and healthcare provider relationships. A descriptive analysis of the concepts of depression, substance abuse, abuse, and sexual ownership were conducted. Scores from questions that measured each concept were consolidated into four separate composite variables. Correlations between composite variables were conducted. Statistically significant relationships were found between abuse with depression, substance use and abuse, the number of sexual partners and the number of unprotected sexual partners. Additionally a negative relationship between abuse and sexual ownership was found. The results support other studies that show a relationship between abuse and high risk behaviors, such as, drug use, number of sexual partners, depression, low levels of sexual ownership, and STDs.

Introduction/Background

Research indicates that abuse is associated with severe psychological, emotional, and behavioral damage. It can inhibit the survivor from living a healthy, happy, and productive life. Victims differ in the extent to which they suffer from abuse. It depends on the severity of the abuse. The support and help received after the disclosure are also important factors. Sexual abuse affects approximately one in three female adolescents, and it is particularly traumatic (Ohene, 2005). There is evidence for the effects of abuse on depression, self-esteem, substance abuse, physical abuse and high numbers of sexual partners (Daniels, De Arellano, Ehrenreich, Suarez, Bennett, Cheron, Goldstein, Jakle, Landon & Trosper, 2006).

Depression

Depression is a mood disorder; and it is characterized by a "low state marked by significant levels of sadness, lack of energy, low self-worth, as well as guilt" (Comer, 2007). It is associated with both a history of abuse and history of STI (Etier, Kershaw, Lewis, Milan, Niccolai & Ickovics, 2006). Since sexual risk behaviors are associated with individuals who have experienced abuse, and depression, the depression and STI's may be a resulting co-morbidity as a result of the abuse. Abuse victims have been more likely diagnosed with depressive and stress symptoms and disorders, such as, post traumatic stress disorders than those who have not experienced abuse as a child due to the intense trauma they experienced as children (Danielson et al., 2006). STI's are also linked with stress disorders. Post traumatic stress disorder, one of the anxiety disorders, results from stress inducing situations, such as, a traumatic event, and when the symptoms continue a month or more after the event (Comer 2007).

Substance Abuse

Substance abuse is defined by Comer (2007) as "a pattern of behavior in which people rely on a drug excessively and regularly, bringing damage to their relationships, functioning poorly at work, or putting themselves or others in danger." Victims of abuse are often said to be more likely to use illicit drugs as means of coping with the traumatic event (Danielson et al., 2006). According to Danielson (2006), "females receiving treatment for substance abuse are approximately twice as likely to report a history of child sexual abuse." Stressful life events have been found to result in higher rates of drug use among female victims of abuse (Widom & Marmorstein, 2006). Compared with individuals who have not experienced abuse, victims of abuse are more likely to report substance use in adulthood after their twenties, in which drug use is still considered experimental (Widom & Marmorstein 2006). The use of drugs and alcohol can cause severe future health problems, such as kidney and liver failure, diabetes, high blood pressure, and heart disease. Further, the use of drugs is illegal, and adolescents are potentially harming their future if they are caught and become identified as a juvenile delinquent in the criminal justice system. Their use influences the adolescent's ability to fulfill educational obligations, such as, studying and attending classes that could end in their eventually dropping out of high school. The result can be decreased work and economic stability which may increase depression, substance use, and criminal justice recidivism as adults if they were caught as adolescents.

Number of Sexual Partners

Being a victim of child sexual abuse is associated with having a higher number of sexual partners than those who haven't been abused because sexual intercourse may come to be used to meet a need for attention and affection. Further, they may engage in sexual behaviors earlier in life than non-victims, which may account for a larger life-time count of sexual partners (Testa, VanZile-Tamsen & Livingston, 2005). Abused women may continually seek relationships that result in more abuse, due to a lack of boundaries and assertiveness, plus a subconscious pattern originating from the abuse where they involve themselves in abusive relationships. The lack of quality relationships therefore, may be leading to a greater quantity (Testa et. al., 2005). The time in which the abuse occurs is also during the time in which social norms are learned, which may result in the behavior being misinterpreted and modeled as a normative behavior. Sexual promiscuity may serve as a means for socializing with the opposite sex, and result in high numbers of sexual partners (Ohene, 2005).

Trust

Women who have experienced abuse have a difficult time trusting both themselves as well as others. Being unable to protect them from abuse in the past leads the victims to a sense of vulnerability for the future. This lack of trust has implications for future relationships. Because relationships are built on trust, those that lack trust are less likely to succeed. This failure to maintain stable relationships may also add to the continuous cycle of unsuccessful relationships that lead to higher numbers of partners (Champion & Shaun, 1998). Also, women that were abused as children were not protected by important people in their primary group such as parents or relatives. The inability to save oneself, and the lack of a protecting person, leaves the women feeling vulnerable to future abuse and may be more inclined to retreat from situations such as relationships that require trust, or engage in frequent non-serious relationships that do not require trust or commitment, contributing to the high total number of partners.

Sexual Ownership

Sexual ownership refers to sexual assertiveness and sexual rights. According to East and Adams (2002), "To be assertive means to pursue one's goals, or to state them with assurance and self-confidence." It includes the power to identify one's sexual desires and to refuse unwanted sexual advances (East & Adams 2002).

The consequences of sexual abuse include the survivor's loss of personal space boundaries (Geanellos, 2003). Identification of oneself as an object of another's desire often occurs among sexual abuse victims who become less likely to understand their own worth and value, including the ability to identify where the self begins and ends in relation to another.

These women were abused early in adolescents or childhood at a time when they are still forming their identity. Abuse interrupts the development of personal and sexual identity, resulting in boundaries that are open and vulnerability to exploitive relationships (Geanellos, 2003). Feeling that she is an object for someone else's pleasure affects empowerment to use a condom and decision making pertaining to the possible consequences, such as, pregnancy and getting tested for STD's. Further, assertiveness with regard to sexual self satisfaction may take a backseat to the sexual satisfaction of others (East & Adams 2002). Sexual ownership is thus related to sexual education and understanding of sexual desire.

Methods

General Design of the Research

The researcher along with another intern continued previous work of a previous research assistant. The research was a secondary analysis of a subset of an ongoing National Institute of Drug Abuse grant funded research program through the University of Texas at The San Antonio School of Medicine under the direction of Dr. Jane Dimmit Champion. The researcher spent the summer of 2008 interning with this team. Permission to conduct a secondary analysis and publish the findings was granted by the principal investigators. This study is a control-randomized trial of African- and Mexican-American adolescent females who have a history of sexually transmitted infection (STI) and/or abuse. This analysis was conducted to explore the association of participants' sexual risk behaviors, substance use, and psychosocial elements of depression and sexual ownership. A literature review on abuse, depression, substance abuse, and STI prevalence among adolescents was conducted. The data were entered into the computer using Statistical Package for the Social Sciences (SPSS) and gathered through administration of the study interview tool. Insight into the participants was gained as a result of the interview experience with the cases, most of whom experienced some sort of abuse, and history of STI.

The analyses focused on exploring how depression, low sexual ownership, high numbers of sexual partners, and drug usage may be associated with the abuse. There were three interviews: a baseline, a six month and twelve month follow-up interview. Medical exams were also conducted. Incentives included money and free medicines for sexual health and birth control.

Operationalization and Data Collection

A semi-structured interview was administered to the participants and it contained the Rosenberg Self-Esteem Scale that was used to determine participant's level of depression and self-esteem. The scale consists of twenty questions. Each question was scored on a Likert Scale from one to four; the higher the score the lower the participant's self-esteem and depression. So that all of the scoring would be consistent, the coding of four questions where the higher score represented high self esteem was reversed. The depression scores between 20-40 represented normal limits. Scores from 41-60 were representative of mild depression, and a score of 61-80 was considered very depressed. The composite variable that represented the concept of abuse combined scores from 27 questions. Eleven questions referred to physical or emotional abuse, and sixteen referred to sexual abuse. There were twelve questions referring to various drug use in the last thirty days of the participant's interview, that were combined to create the substance abuse composite score. The sexual ownership composite score was based on six questions that referenced assertiveness with condom use, declining unwanted sexual advances, and knowledge of sexual desires.

Selection of the Cases

The 250 female participants between the ages of thirteen to nineteen were either referred by local sexual health clinics in San Antonio, Texas for having a history of previous or current sexually transmitted infection, or the girls themselves referred friends and relatives.

Analysis

Exploratory analyses of the data were conducted using SPSS frequencies for descriptive analyses and Pearson Correlation Coefficient to examine the strength of the association between abuse, depression, sexual ownership, and substance abuse. Of the 250 girls, 74.4% (186) identified themselves as Hispanic, 17.2% (43) of the total as African American, 3.2% (8) of the total as both African American and Hispanic, 3.6% (9) of the total as Hispanic and 4.4% (11) as other. Of the 250 participants 80.4 percent (201) answered yes to at least one of the sexual, physical, or emotional abuse questions in the survey; these participants were further analyzed to find relationships between the abuse and their behavior, depression scores, and sexual assertiveness.

Results

The data from this analysis support other evidence that links a history of abuse with other risk behaviors, such as, substance use and risky sexual behavior, as well as, with other emotional components, such as, depression and sexual ownership. A low, but statistically significant association was demonstrated between abuse and recent drug use ($r = .172$, $p<.01$). This showed that those participants that experienced at least one type of abuse were likely to have used some type of drug within thirty days previous to their participation in the interview. A low, but significant correlation was also found between history of abuse and depression ($r =.202$, $p<.01$). Participants who experienced abuse were also likely to have higher levels of depression and lower self-esteem. A low to moderate, but significant correlation was also found between history of abuse and the total number of sexual partners, (r=.333, p<.01). Additionally, a low to moderate correlation that was significant was found in the total number of unprotected sexual partners, (r=.349, p<.01). These last two comparisons showed the highest correlations. This association with unprotected sex may also help to understand the high rates of STI found among individuals with a history of abuse. There was a low to moderate inverse association between abuse and sexual ownership (r=-.306, p<.01). This suggests that abuse participants are not likely to have sexual ownership, and thus more likely to participate in risky sexual behaviors which may also explain the high numbers of unprotected sexual partners and history of STDs.

Table 1
Correlation of Sexual Abuse
With
Ownership, Drug Use, Parners, Depression, and Unsafe Sex

Variable	At least one type of sexual abuse	Sig.	n
Sexual Ownership	-.306**	.000	201
Recent Drug Use	.172**	.007	241
Total number of male partners ever had sex with	.333**	.000	250
Total depression score	.202**	.002	237
Total number of partners (had unprotected sex with)	.349**	.000	244

**Significant at the .01 level (2-tailed test)

Discussion

These preliminary exploratory analyses between drug use and abuse support other studies where higher rates of drug use were found among individuals who had experienced child abuse, whether physical or sexual (Kilpatrick, 2003). It is important that the issue of drug usage in abuse victims be addressed not only because they do harm to the user's body and it is a criminal offense, but it also impairs judgment. Impaired judgment can influence the individual's ability to require condom use, or turn down sexual advances putting them at a greater risk for acquiring an STI. The association of depression and abuse is supported by other studies that identified higher levels of depression

with victims of child abuse (Kawsar, Walters & Foster, 2004).

The inverse relationship between abuse and sexual ownership may be explained by the positive association of abuse with number of sexual partners and unprotected sexual partners. The abuse may be associated with less assertiveness with one's sexual health, responsibility, and understanding of personal pleasure. Low sexual ownership may explain high numbers of sexual partners, and unprotected sexual partners. Participants may be less likely to say no to unwanted sexual advances, require condom use during sexual intercourse, and negotiate precautions necessary for their health and well being with regard to STDs and birth control. The sexual experience may be more focused on the desires of the partner than that of the participants (Merill, Guimond, Thomsen & Milner, 2003).

As suggested by other evidence, women with a history of abuse are at risk for engaging in other unsafe health practices (Champion & Shane 1998). The sample consisted of racial/ethnic minority girls from low socioeconomic backgrounds, and the results may differ in higher socioeconomic backgrounds, among male abuse victims, and other populations. The influence of culture on the participants' behaviors and beliefs in regard to sexual behaviors and female assertiveness needs further exploration. The majority of the sample in this study were Hispanic, non- white females (approximately 75 percent). The Hispanic community is known for having a machismo, patriarchal culture in which the male is more dominant and the woman is more submissive and less assertive. Culture may be an influential dynamic in understanding the behavioral patterns of this population in regard to sexual assertiveness.

The results may only be generalizable to racial/ethnic minority populations with low socioeconomic backgrounds. The associations found were consistent with findings from other studies. Interventions such as those implemented by the primary research study that included workshops about sexual education and sexual health, one on one counseling, and support groups are important for combating the behaviors associated with abuse victims that may negatively affect their health and well being. The researcher believes that other counseling sessions should focus on changing irrational cognitive thinking that may contribute to the participation in risky behaviors (which may have resulted in low self-esteem and depression as a consequence of the abuse). If these girls are told that they are responsible for the abuse, or that they are worthless and treated like property they may begin to subconsciously identify with these ideas as truths and it can become a self-fulfilling prophecy. Future research should explore the results of support these victims had in order to determine whether or not it can have an influence on combating risky behaviors. Other studies could exam those survivors who did not engage in risky behaviors in order to ascertain what can positively influence survivors to live healthy and well balanced lives. Risk behaviors identified must be addressed in both research and applied in relationships with healthcare providers in order to better assist these individuals.

References

Champion, Jane Dimmitt, & Shain, Rochelle. (1998). The context of sexually transmitted disease: life histories of woman abuse: *Issues in Mental Health Nursing*, 19, 463- 480.

Comer, Ronald J. (2007). *Abnormal Psychology* (6th Ed.). New York, NY: Worth.

Danielson, Carla Kmett, De Arellano, Michael A., Ehrenreich, Jill T., Suarez, Liza M.,

Bennett, Shannon M., Cheron, Daniel M., Goldstein, Clark R., M.A., Jakle, Katherine R., Landon, Terri M., & Trosper, Sarah E., (2006). Identification of high-risk behaviors among victimized adolescents and implications for empirically supported psychosocial treatment: *Journal of Psychiatric Practice*, 12, 364-383.

East, Patricia, & Adams, Joyce. (2002). Sexual assertiveness and adolescents' sexual rights: *Perspectives on Sexual and Reproductive Health*, 43, 212-213.

Etier, Kathleen A., Kershaw, Trace S., Lewis, Jessica B., , Milan,

Stephanie, Niccolai, Linda M. & Ickovics, Jeannette R. (2006) Self-esteem, emotional distress and sexual behavior among adolescents females: Inter-

relationships and temporal effects: *Journal of Adolescent Health*, 38, 268-274.

Fitzpatrick, Kevin M., Wright, Darlene R., Piko, Bettina F.& LaGory, Mark (2005).

Depressive symptomatology, exposure to violence, and the role of social capital among African American adolescents: *American Journal of Orthopsychiatry*, 75, 262-274.

Geanellos, Rene (2003). Understanding the need for personal space boundary restoration in women-client survivors of intrafamilial childhood sexual abuse: *International Journal of Mental Health Nursing*, 12, 186-193.

Hills, Susan D., Anda, Robert F., Felitti, Vincent J., & Marchbanks, Polly A. (2001).

Adverse childhood experiences and sexual risk behaviors in women: a retrospective cohort study: *Family Planning Perspectives*, 33, 206-211.

Kawsar, M., Anfield, A., Walters, E., McCabe, S., & Forster G.E. (2004). Prevalence of

Sexually transmitted infection and mental health needs of female child and adolescent survivors of rape and sexual assault attending a specialist clinic: *Sexually Transmitted Infections*, 80, 138-141.

Kilpatrick, Dean G., Ruggiero, Kenneth J., Acierno, Ron, Saunders, Benjamin E.,

Resnick, Heidi S., & Best, Connie L. (2003). Violence and risk of PTSD, major

Depression, substance abuse/ dependence, and comorbidity: results from the

National survey of adolescent: *Journal of Consulting and Clinical Psychology*, 71, 692-700.

Merril, Lex L., Guimond, Jennifer M., Thomsen, Cynthia J., & Milner, Joel S. (2003).

Child sexual abuse and number of sexual partners in young women: the role of abuse severity, coping style, and sexual functioning: *Journal of Consulting and Clinical Psychology*, 7, 987-996.

Morrow, K. Brent, & Sorell, Gwendolyn T. (1989). Factors affecting self-esteem,

Depression and negative behaviors in sexually abused female adolescents: *Journal of Marriage and Family*, 51, 677-686.

Ohene, Sally-Ann, Halcon, Linda, Ireland, Marjorie, Carr, Peter & McNeely,

Clea (2005). Sexual abuse history, risk behavior, and sexually transmitted diseases: the impact of age at abuse: *Sexually Transmitted Diseases*, 32, 358-363.

Parillo, Kathleen M., Freeman, Robert C., Collier, Karyn, & Young, Paul (2001).

Association between early sexual abuse and adult HIV risky sexual behaviors among community-recruited women: *Child Abuse & Neglect*, 25, 335-346.

Testa, Maria, VanZile-Tamsen, Carol, Livingston, Jennifer A. (2005). Childhood Sexual

abuse, relationship satisfaction, and sexual risk taking in a community sample of

women: *Journal of Consulting and Clinical Psychology*, 73, 1116-1124.

Widom, Cathy Spatz, Marmorstein, Naomi (2006). Childhood victimization and illicit

drug use in middle adulthood: *Psychology of Addictive Behaviors*, 20, 394-403.

The Formal and Informal Behavior of Psychiatric Clients in Institution Z: A Field Study

Leticia Garza
Senior, Psychology Major

(Dr. Debra L. Murphy, Major Advisor for Psychology)

For many years the phenomena of clients' behaviors in psychiatric settings have been in great question. Research has indicated that clients' behaviors in formal settings differ from their behaviors in informal settings because the settings in the formal environment shape the clients' behaviors momentarily. This observational analysis was based on an eleven-week field study of nineteen patients in a mental institution, which will be referred to as Institution Z. The top three diagnoses found among the participants being observed in the areas that were focused on were schizophrenia, bipolar, and major depression. Consistent with previous studies in the research literature, observations made in class settings, quad, and in client environments had predictable patterns of behavior depending on whether it was a week day or weekend and were reflective of setting context, e.g., formal versus informal.

Introduction

The purpose of this study was to explore why clients behave one way in one setting and a different way in another setting in an attempt to replicate findings from studies by other researchers. Staff behavior was also observed and recorded. It explored observations of clients' behaviors in formal versus informal settings (class and module sessions), and the role that staff and therapists may play in the perception of the clients' behaviors behind their glass windows. What can be said about the client, or for that matter, about the nurse? Can certain behaviors go misdiagnosed because of the lack of communication with the clients? Institution Z and most mental institutions have a mission statement that focuses on "delivering evidence-based mental health treatment to increase the rates of mental health and wellness."

The promotion of recovery commonly incorporates the method of behavior modification in which a desired behavior is reinforced through provision of tokens that can be exchanged for a desired reward (such as, healthy snacks or perhaps an extra phone call). This method is often used to promote class attendance, improved behavior, and overall discharge. However, tokens were predominately administered right after the achieved behavior in formal settings (before and after class, and after meals and snacks) leaving the informal setting without promotion of recovery. This behavioral modification focus was the ultimate strategy of Institution Z. Ladislav Holy (1984) a researcher of many fields once said,

> *The researcher does not participate in the lives of subjects in order to observe them, but rather observes while participating fully in their lives...through living with the people being studied. She comes to share the same meanings with them in the process of active participation in their social lives. Research means, in this sense, socialization to the culture being studied.*

This researcher's observations were not done behind a glass window but rather by engaging in client activities and sharing their emotions in a locked facility. That is what this study was about.

Literature Review

Many studies have been written on the issue relating behaviors by psychiatric clients to their settings. A critical evaluation on a psychiatric ward was done by Constonis (1966) whose research mentions several things about the system in a mental hospital. Here for example he says,

> *The increasing concern with social structural factors affecting the treatment process of the hospitalized mental client has led to a reconsideration of the organization of services provided for clients in these settings.*

An interesting point that Constonis (1966) made is that the unit is supposed

to be a fraction of the whole, meaning that the unit represents a smaller representation of the hospital. He then goes on to say:

> *Yet there is a growing conviction among practitioners that environmental factors play an important role, both positive and negative, in the experiences of the client while he is hospitalized.*

In addition, the researcher read over the research by Banks (1956). His study helped to modify this researcher's observations in the units. His observations lead him to say:

> *Staff members were able to discuss clients in terms of symptoms and overt behavior, especially behavior that caused extra work for the staff. To secure reliable data concerning client social structure, it was necessary to resort to simple observation of client behavior.*

Through his gathering of information he was able to create a map representing the clients' setting and the placements of clients' seating. In accordance with this study, Skipper, et. al. (1964) made a hypothesis about staff behavior towards clients' communication.

> *The greater the pressure on hospital functions to achieve the instrumental goals of care and cure, the less the probability they will communicate with clients except when it is defined as instrumental for care and cure.*

This makes an excellent point toward the observations made in the settings of

Institution Z. According to the research of Melbin (1969):

> *Clients in a small private mental hospital behave crazily much more often on weekdays than they do on evenings or weekends. They also show disturbance on evenings and weekends, but during these periods, such upsets are to be very normal in form. This difference implies that the expression of mental disturbance has to do with the environment in which it happens.*

Melbin's (1969) finding on unusual behavior makes significant points on how the clients' rhythms should be observed. He states:

> *On occasion healthy individuals do act strangely. It is about their frequency in our society. It is common to hit someone or kick a chair but unusual to the frequency, the repetitive enactment of an usual repertoire, or the severity of a given performance, that leads to branding the actors crazy and consigning them to mental hospitals.*

According to the research of Rosenhan (1973),

> *Once a person is designated abnormal, all of his other behaviors and characteristics are colored by that label.*

However, certain behaviors are modified in psychiatric settings because either their reinforcement is continuous or any behavior is reinforced. Certain methods of reinforcement are effective if used correctly in psychiatric settings. In addition, communication is important in effective client care and staff members should be more courteous in their contact with clients on a one to one level. According to the research on the perceptions of how dangerous clients are conducted by Brockman, et al. (1978),

> *One consistent finding is that individuals who have had contact with the mentally ill are less likely to endorse social distancing responses towards them.*

It takes staff communication with clients to understand if their behavior is being slowly modified by their reinforcements or if other measures have to be taken rather than standing behind a glass window.

Methods

Client and staff behaviors were observed according to time, setting, week day and weekend. Clients' behaviors were observed from 9 a.m. to 9 p.m. during week days however clients' behaviors during the weekend were observed solely on unit behavior between noon and 9 p.m. A scale that rated behavior on a scale of 1 to 5 was used to monitor clients' behaviors in class settings.

Rating Behavior
1 meaning formal behavior
3 meaning moderate behavior
5 meaning informal behavior

Settings: Classroom= Formal Structure
Courtyard = Informal Structure
Unit = Informal Structure

Formal behavior was defined as:
- Respectful of others
- Quite during lecture
- Paying attention
- Participate in activity
- Raise hand to be acknowledged
- Be aware
- Not letting the voices overtake a persons behavior
- Hygiene
- Appropriate Conversations

Informal behavior was defined as:
- Walking around talking to yourself
- Inappropriate hygiene
- Engaging in inappropriate conversations or behavior with others
- Relaxing in chair watching T.V.
- Drawing, coloring, sleeping playing cards or any leisure time games
- Phone conversation with nobody
- Out bursts of behavior
- Talking to Psychiatric Nursing Assistant's (PNA) about yourself or general topics
- Talking to volunteer
- Anything not tolerated in class

A social map of the rhythms during their stay in the ward was also used for behavioral analysis. However, two maps of the unit had to be developed to measure the clients' behavior on weekdays and weekends. This social map monitored sixteen clients in their informal setting. This social map has nine colors to mark the areas where clients usually hang out during the weekday and weekend. A convenience sample of sixteen was used based on their availability in the ward that was observed.

Field notes were additionally used to monitor behaviors. These notes consisted of clients' breakdowns, confessions, emotions, thoughts of their illness, and staff behavior. These notes marked clients' behaviors before and after administration of medicine and many other things. Clients were given numbers to protect their confidentiality:

1. Religious Guy
2. Government Guy
3. Eye Shadow Lady
4. Young Smirker
5. Attitude Woman
6. New Guy
7. Trans Guy
8. Jacket Guy
9. Depression Lady
10. Crazy Curly
11. High Guy
12. Matrix Girl
13. Curly Cat Guy
14. Loud Guy
15. Stare Lady
16. Midlife Lady
17. ET Lady
18. Cowgirl
19. Mom Lady

***Clients 6, 7, and 18 were from another unit.

Figure 1
Social Map (Blank)

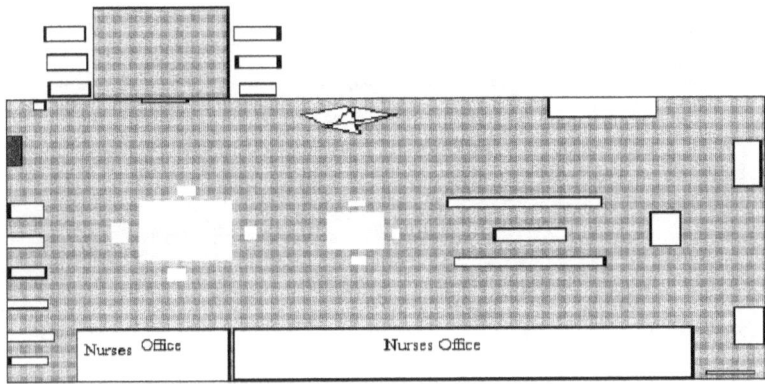

Results

The results presented in the unit are dramatically different from the class setting. The social map marked the rhythms of the clients during a weekday. However, Map 3 taken during the weekend unquestionably demonstrated the difference in the clients' behavior rhythms.

1. Religious Guy
2. Government Guy
3. Eye Shadow Lady
4. Young Smirker
5. Attitude Woman
6. New Guy
7. Trans Guy
8. Jacket Guy
9. Depression Lady
10. Crazy Curly
11. High Guy
12. Matrix Girl
13. Curly Cat Guy
14. Loud Guy
15. Stare Lady
16. Midlife Lady
17. ET Lady
18. Cowgirl
19. Mom Lady

Figure 2
Social Map (Weekdays)

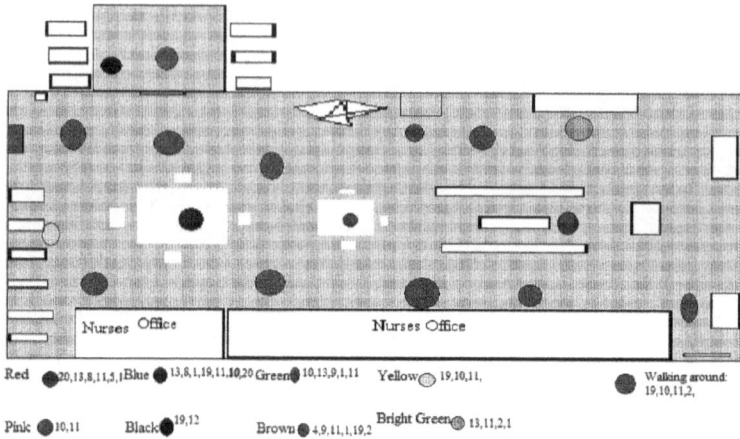

Green highlights indicate that the clients' behavior was observed in class session or in the court yard however, unit observation was not initiated for these three clients.

Figure 3
Social Map 3 of Unit on Weekends

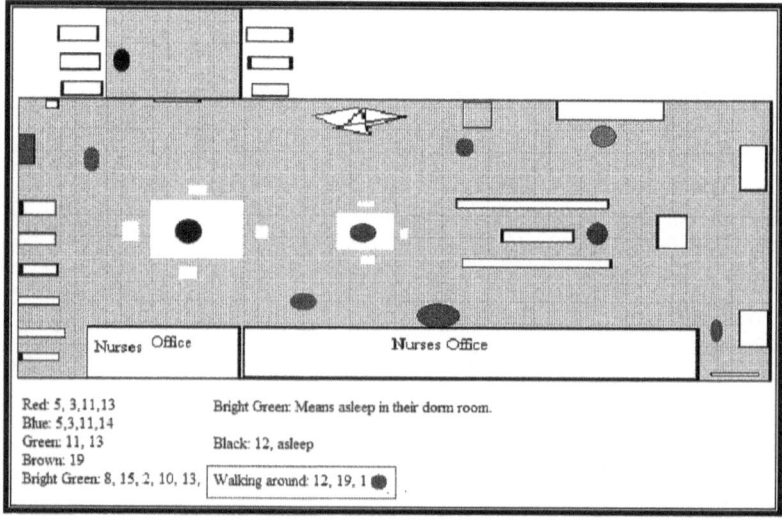

This chart demonstrates a low active setting in the units during the weekend.

1. Religious Guy
2. Government Guy
3. Eye Shadow Lady
4. Young Smirker
5. Attitude Woman
6. New Guy
7. Trans Guy
8. Jacket Guy
9. Depression Lady
10. Crazy Curly
11. High Guy
12. Matrix Girl
13. Curly Cat Guy
14. Loud Guy
15. Stare Lady
16. Midlife Lady
17. ET Lady
18. Cowgirl
19. Mom Lady

The difference between Maps 2 and 3 is that Map 2 has clients very active through the day in the unit, however Map 3 shows decreases because the activity throughout the unit has decreased and has caused more clients to sleep. Another surprising observation made in the unit maps was that 95 % of the staff was to themselves rather than communicating with the clients.

The purple dots located in Maps 2 and 3 shed light on the excess amount of anxiety found in a locked facility. Clients 19, 10, 11, 2, and this researcher/observer had to walk around because of the lack of activities and communication. Staff behind the glass windows noted this behavior as *manic behavior* yet this researcher/observer

wasn't being manic but trying to get the jitters out from being locked in a facility.

Map 3 demonstrates that weekends are less active with any kind of activities or interaction with clients. This researcher/observer often tried bringing extra blank sheets of paper so the clients could engage in a game of tic-tac-toe or drawing. During the weekends staff members were usually sitting around waiting for an incident to happen and efforts to interact with the clients were very minimal.

Map 2 demonstrated an active work week with the clients and staff members. This supported the research by Melbins (1969). He was correct in the sense that clients are more likely to act up during a weekday than a weekend. Clients know they can get more attention during the week because of the amount of staff around to cater to their needs. As to weekends there were no classes to attend or activities therefore, a client is left with a hand full of choices to act on during the day.

Several clients would change their attitudes once this researcher/observer came into the unit with them. For example, clients 13, 8, 1, 19, 11, 20 would stop walking around and sit with the researcher/observer at the table to talk or draw. The simplest amount of attention would dramatically change their behavior.

Table 1 was designed to monitor the behavior of clients in their class settings.

Table 1
Chart of Behavior in Class Settings

Class observations	Morning Ratings	Afternoon Ratings	Other Observations
	Informal 90 %/	Informal 80%	
Monday Sept. 18	Formal 10%	Formal 20 %	
	Informal 90 %	Informal 50%	
Friday Sept. 22	Formal 10%	Formal 50%	
	Informal 90 %	Informal 50%	
Monday Sept. 25	Formal 10%	Formal 50 %	
	Informal 90 %	Informal 90%	
Friday Sept. 29	Formal 10%	Formal 10%	
	Informal 50%	Informal 50%	
Monday, Oct. 2	Formal 50%	Formal 50%	1 Outburst
	Informal 50%	Informal 50%	
Friday, Oct. 6	Formal 50%	Formal 50%	
	Informal 10%	Formal 10%	
Monday, Oct. 9	Formal 90%	Informal 90%	
	Informal 30%	Informal 50%	
Friday, Oct. 13	Formal 70%	Formal 50%	
	Informal 90%	Informal 50%	
Monday, Oct. 16	Formal 10%	Formal 50%	2 outbursts
	Informal 90%	Informal 90%	
Friday, Oct. 20	Formal 10%	Formal 10%	3 outbursts
	Informal 40%	Informal 40%	
Monday, Oct. 23	Formal 60%	Formal 60%	
	Informal 20%	Informal 40%	
Friday, Oct. 27	Formal 80%	Formal 60%	4 outbursts
	all day in unit 100 %		
Saturday, Oct. 28	informal	all day in unit 100 %	
	Informal 40%		
Monday, Oct. 30	Formal 60%	100% formal	
	Informal 40%	Informal 20%	
Friday, Nov. 3	Formal 60%	Formal 80%	
		all day in unit 100%	
Saturday, Nov. 4	100% informal	informal	
	Informal 50%	Informal 50%	
Monday, Nov. 13	Formal 50%	Formal 50%	
Monday, Nov. 20	100 % formal	100 % formal	
	Informal 80%	Informal 90%	
Friday, Nov. 24	Formal 20%	Formal 10%	
Monday, Nov. 27	100% formal	100% formal	
Friday, Dec. 1	100% formal	100% formal	

The four incidents were recorded in a formal setting and the majority of the behavior of the clients favored formal behavior. The class setting had more of a controlled environment however their reinforcement towards the clients varied. Clients are only allowed to receive tokens when they attend class on time and stay throughout the session. Clients in these sessions received tokens when they arrived late and left early. Some clients left early but received tokens if some work got done. The staff were not rewarding continuous desired behavior (as they were supposed to), but they were rewarding any behavior. Therefore, they did not promote recovery for these clients. In addition, the formal settings are a bit more structured; however, clients manipulated their behavior for their reward. If he or she must only meet certain criteria to receive tokens, they seemed to do just enough to meet their criteria and it seemed that their unit behavior was truly their behavior.

Discussion

The researcher's observation saw many things wrong with the setting. Lack of funding was constantly blamed for the deficiencies in therapeutic techniques. However, communicating with clients doesn't require extra money or for that matter time. If staff could spend a total of four hours sitting down and watching T.V. in the unit then perhaps they can spread that time and talk with their clients. This researcher/observer came on Saturdays to spend time with the clients, not because she had to, but because she wanted to. She learned so much from them and felt what they felt; being in a contained place with no life. Research has proven that little modifications to your settings can dramatically change the attitudes and behaviors of clients without spending a dime.

Another disturbing action this researcher witnessed was with a staff member and client #12. Client 12 kept on cussing so staff would deliberately take the client's jacket away every time she cussed. Client 12 knew all she had to do was stop cussing and she'd get her jacket back. Staff A must have taken the jacket away over nine times in one night. Positive reinforcement, according to research, would have been a more effective approach toward changing behavior.

Client 5 constantly had an attitude toward one rehab therapist, in particular, but this researcher's observations suggested that the therapist was agitating the client. However, to Client 5 or any other client, this researcher/observer was no different than they were because this researcher/observer didn't have much authority to do anything for them. Client 5 constantly wanted to talk to this researcher/observer and play cards. She was an additional one, among other clients who didn't interact with anybody.

Client 8 was a kind client. Yes, he had his psychotic episode while off medications but once he became stabilized he was able to carry a good conversation. Client 8 is the reason why staff should communicate with the clients. Client 8's family disowned him after they learned of his illness and he's been homeless since 16. Client 8 has no visitors and the fact that he doesn't, makes him depressed. He once said to me, "Are you here to help us? Because if you are then I'm glad... it's good to talk to someone every now and then especially when you don't have family that cares to visit or call." Client 8's comment made this researcher/observer feel good because not all clients are fortunate enough to have somebody to care for them and that is why volunteers are there...for them.

References

Banks, P.E., (1956). Methodological problems in the study of psychiatric wards. *Social Forces*, Vol. 34, No. 3. 278.

Brockman, J., D'Arcy, C.; Edmonds, L., 1979; Facts or artifacts? Changing public attitudes towards the mentally ill, Social Science and Medicine. Part A: *Medical Psychology & Medical Sociology*, 13: 673-682.

Costonis, Anthony F., (1966). The mental hospital unit system: a critical evaluation and research statement. *Journal of Health and Human Behavior*, Vol. 7, No. 2. 75-83.

Holy, Ladislav; and Stuchik, Milan, *Actions, Norms and Representations: Foundations of Anthropological Enquiry*, First Edition, Boston, Mass., CambridgeUniversity Press, 1984.

Melbin, Murray, Behavior rhythms in mental hospitals (1969), *The American Journal of Sociology*, Vol. 74, No. 6, 650.

Rosenhan, L. David, On being sane in insane places (1973). *Science*, 179: 250- 258.

Skipper, James K. Jr., Tagliacozzo, Daisy L., Mauksch, Hans, What communication means to patients (1964), *American Journal of Nursing*, 64:101-103

Dual Diagnosis and Homelessness in Austin, Texas: Are Programs and Institutions Effective in Assisting Citizens with Adequate Support?

Divina M. Ormsby
Senior, Psychology

(Dr. Debra L. Murphy, Major Advisor for Psychology)

Abstract

This researcher/observer examined the effectiveness of programs designed to end chronic homelessness for individuals with a co-occurring mental illness and addiction to illegal substances. Statistical rates of homelessness and quality of programming available to this subpopulation of clients in a town in Texas and other major cities in the nation were compared and contrasted. The researcher observed, recorded, and analyzed data from two client case studies at a mental institution in a town in Texas to provide insight into what programs work best for these clients. The researcher/observer also examined the amount and quality of services available. Studies from the literature pertaining to the effectiveness and quality of such programming were also reviewed. This research showed that services for the homeless in the Austin metropolitan area incorporate some successful techniques that are used in many other programs across the nation that deal with homelessness. However, there is a lack of programs available with a high success rate for those with a co-occurring mental illness and illegal substance addiction. These individuals naturally fall victim to homelessness and life on the streets. The defining factors working against effective programming were found to be structural and personal obstacles in getting government support rather than particular inefficiencies within a specific program. Programs nationwide have had difficulty caring for those who are homeless with a dual diagnosis.

Introduction

Many scholars and modern philosophers believe that America's social setback concerning homelessness issues is a great national embarrassment for what is supposed to be the most developed and powerful nation in the world. There is occurring a structural transformation across the nation, including all of the major cities, which helps contribute to the rising number of people becoming homeless. America's economic structure is focusing less on manufacturing and more on information and services. According to an article written by Steven Segaller (1999), corporations have moved their plants to other states and other countries. The number of well paying jobs for skilled workers diminished as a result. Another apparent cause of homelessness in America, and cities like Austin, are the rates of citizens not having an adequate income, affordable housing, and proper health insurance. America is one of the few developed countries in the world that hasn't implemented a universal health care system. It is increasingly more expensive to pay for health care on a national level. Also, health insurance is only obtainable and beneficial for those who have enough money. The number of uninsured people in America is staggering. In 2003, the U.S. Census Bureau recorded that 15.6 percent of Americans were uninsured. That equates to about 45 million people. Across the nation a lack of affordable and supportive housing has caused major homelessness. Some theorists may explain the high occurrence of homelessness on the country's dismissal of spirituality. Not like in other smaller countries, America separates religion from state. Many philosophers believe that spirituality and religion create stability in ethics and moral order. More recently, some argue that people who live in the streets choose to be homeless. It's based on the idea that because of some people's personality and upbringing, they cannot and choose not to fit into mainstream society.

The capitalist society that upholds the principles of upward mobility and economic success often leaves the individuals who don't represent the majority in the dust. Including these individuals who are left behind are those who struggle with a mental illness and addiction. It has been found that programs designed to help the homeless on a grand scale actually have not helped those dealing with dual diagnosis and homelessness as much. There is great importance in understanding the lives of individuals with a mental illness and substance abuse problem. Society often blames the victim with a mental illness for his or her drug and homelessness problem. Families often give up on those who are dealing with a mental illness and addiction. Finding work, affordable housing, and health insurance is even more difficult for those with severe psychotic disorders, as mainstream society has difficulty meeting their needs. There is a crippling stigma that follows those with a mental illness, and substance abuse just worsens the situation. America must understand homelessness and dual-diagnosis because homelessness cannot be cured. It is basically the natural result of drug abuse and mental illness. More importantly, plans to alleviate homelessness in the Austin metropolitan area for those with a dual diagnosis should be reorganized and developed. Questions arise on whether the programs for homelessness and support systems in the Austin metropolitan area are relatively effective, and if so, to what extent do the programs help those with a mental illness?

Defining Chronic Homelessness, Dual Diagnosis, and Revolving Door

Every country, state, and city defines homelessness differently. In Texas, according to the Texas Homeless Network and Department of Housing and Urban Development (2006), chronic homelessness is defined by persons living in places not meant for habitation: streets, emergency shelters, transitional or supportive housing, and mental institutions. Also, those fleeing domestic violence, and being evicted from a home for more than 30 days are considered homeless. For sake of simplicity this research is based on the Department of Housing and Urban Development's (HUD) definitions of homelessness. HUD is a national organization designed to increase homeownership, make access to affordable housing, and support community development. Supportive housing is less costly and helps treat those with a dual diagnosis if they are housed first and then treated (Barrow and Zimmer, 2006).

To understand homelessness relative to dual diagnosis, we must define the phenomenon of dual diagnosis and how professionals have responded to it. In its most basic context dual diagnosis is the co-existence of any psychiatric disorders with a substance use disorder in the same individual (Rassool, 2002). There is debate on the reasons why the mentally ill misuse drugs. Such theories comprise explanations that focus on social drift, deinstitutionalization, self-medication, and common genetic susceptibility, which may predispose to both conditions. Despite the reasons why dual diagnosis exists, substance misuse has been associated with an increased rate of relapse in the chronically mentally ill (Poole & Brabbins, 1996). One of the reasons why it's difficult to alleviate homelessness for individuals with a dual diagnosis is the natural occurrence of relapsing or the revolving door syndrome.

The Texas Homeless Network works to provide information to groups that work directly with the homeless in the state of Texas. According to their interactive website, Community Action Network (CAN) is an organization in the Austin metropolitan area that brainstorms and creates plans for the betterment of local area social, health, and human services. Although these organizations are doing great and helpful things for those who are homeless and mentally stable, do they significantly help the homeless with a dual diagnosis and who are experiencing revolving door trends?

One of the most troubling sights at institutions, such as, Institution X* (on which this research is based) is the occurrence of *revolving door syndrome*. This is when patients are cycled in and out of institutions and life on the street. Homeless persons were 15% of admissions to Institution X in October 2003 (Community Action Network, 2003). It is no secret that the same patients often cycle through mental health institutions for many years, never grasping skills of independent living. If substance abuse tends to be the majority of clients' problems at institutions like Institution X why is it so hard to break people of revolving door syndrome and life on the streets, particularly if they are substance abusers? Some argue that humans are biologically susceptible to substance abuse. This means that humans tend to want to use more drugs after being exposed to it. Just like hunger, sex, and happiness; humans innately desire an *artificial paradise*. Ronald K. Siegel (1989) argues that all species of animals use intoxicating drugs ranging from coffee berries to nectars that give euphoric feelings. Being an expert on psychopharmacology, he believes that society needs better drugs that won't induce such bad effects with mental illnesses. Whatever the cause, it's known that it's extremely difficult to break someone of substance abuse and therefore revolving door patterns, which seem to be inextricably tied with the addiction.

Deinstitutionalization

Since deinstitutionalization in the 1950's for individuals with a mental illness, welfare programs dramatically expanded well into the 1960's. Since then homelessness rates grew for those with a mental illness in the 1980's. The plan to deinstitutionalize clients wasn't followed up with a plan for community support systems. However, presently, efforts to decrease homelessness have focused on individual or specific deterrent means: counseling, support groups, and transitional homes: the effectiveness of which is still in question. Many argue that deinstitutionalization, first proposed by President Kennedy, who actually had an institutionalized sister, may have been one of America's worst social domestic policy failures (Rochefort & Mechanic, 1990).

Changing ideologies as a result of World War II and Nazism contributed to deinstitutionalization. The acceptance of large groups of men with mental illnesses from the armed forces, fiscally strained state mental hospitals and perpetuated deinstitutionalization. The introduction of phenothiazines, a medication to treat schizophrenia, propelled the movement. Because it allowed greater predictability in client behavior, institutions were able to modify its policies. Hospitals had new drugs and were ready to release clients into the community, but they had nowhere to send them. Deinstitutionalization was also accelerated in the 1960's because of greater welfare programs. Additionally, the national social move towards civil rights gave those with a mental illness fewer restrictions and more rights. As a result, it became difficult to be admitted to a hospital and easier to get out (Rochefort & Mechanic, 1990).

The cut back of social programs in the 1980's affected the younger generation of people with a mental illness. Unlike the generation after World War II, this new generation stirred more controversy because of the high incidence of drug abuse, alcohol abuse, crime, and psychoses. Agencies have hesitated to give extended health care to young clients who might need treatment for a lifetime. Those with mental illness have a harder time following bureaucratic processes, which makes it impossible for them to maintain housing, employment, and health care. The stigma of mental illness creates a barrier to social mobility. A large proportion of the homeless have a mental illness. There is a general agreement that homelessness is rising. It was accepted that a quarter and a half of the homeless had a mental illness in 1987 (Mechanic & Rochefort, 1990).

Thomas Szasz, a Hungarian philosopher and psychiatrist, believes that modern institutionalization and psychiatry place too much emphasis on making mental illness like physical disease illness with its required medications.

According to Szasz, psychologists and the government should not involuntarily admit people into an institution because a person may not necessarily be *suffering from delusions*. A person needs to only be contained if he or she is infringing on another person's rights. He also feels that the *mentally ill* should be punished for crimes just as others are (Sullum, 2000).

> *The collaboration between government and psychiatry results in what Szasz calls the "therapeutic state," a system in which disapproved thoughts, emotions, and actions are repressed ("cured") through pseudo medical interventions. Thus illegal drug use, smoking, overeating, gambling, shoplifting, sexual promiscuity, pederasty, rambunctiousness, shyness, anxiety, unhappiness, racial bigotry, unconventional religious beliefs, and suicide are all considered diseases or symptoms of diseases--things that happen to people against their will. Szasz believes this sort of thinking undermines individual responsibility and invites coercive paternalism.*

Szasz has many critics who cite that his idea about the nonexistence of mental illness is not consistent with modern psychiatric theory. It's important to point out Szasz's concepts of mental illness because some people believe that the homeless are on the streets by choice. Recently there was a 2005 documentary, Reversal of Fortune, created by Wayne Powers (2007) who showed what happens when someone gives a homeless man a hundred thousand dollars. Powers randomly picked a man who fit the criteria of homeless, mentally stable, and free of drugs. The beginning of the homeless man's journey seemed hopeful. He bought a car and driver's license, got an apartment, paid off old debts, and revisited his family that never supported him. However, he mismanaged his money and did nothing to try and find a job. The man continued to search for cans and bottles for money, continued to sleep on the floor in his apartment, and never took advantage of his two job offers (Powers, 2007). Any professional in the field of psychology could predict such an outcome. However, this speaks volumes when it comes to how people fit into society. Homelessness is only a problem because it doesn't fit into the idea of how society is structured. Are people really homeless by choice? And if so, why don't some homeless people take advantage of support programs designed to help get them off the street? Some will argue that a lack of affordable housing, health care, and income is associated with homelessness. Even so, when opportunities to get these things are provided, some people still fail, particularly those with a dual diagnosis. At some point an individual is going to have to make a conscious choice that he or she wants help and is ready to get off the streets.

Merely providing someone with money, food, and shelter does not alleviate the problems in their life. This is poignantly expressed in the old adage,

Give a man a fish and he'll eat for a day; teach a man to fish and he'll eat for a lifetime.

What seems to happen in institutions and support programs is that people are given opportunities, but do not have the skills of living independently and off the streets. Like in the documentary by Wayne Powers, no one taught the homeless man how to manage money, the importance of getting a real job, support through spirituality, and social skills. Furthermore, his family and new wife abandoned him as soon as his money ran out. He had virtually no support group. It would be even more difficult of a task to get a person with a dual-diagnosis to really internalize independent living skills within a state institution. What occurs at institutions such as Institution X is that some clients never grasp what the therapists teach. Nor do they benefit from the services provided by external programs that are there to help in time of crisis. For many reasons therapy groups aren't as effective in state institutions. People are at their height of disorientation upon admittance, they are in the process of detoxification, on medication that hasn't taken effect yet, experiencing bad side effects, and under emotional trauma. Added to that, many people don't have a place to go after discharge, because their families have turned their backs on them. Homelessness for people with a dual-diagnosis and no support is an issue that seems to get glossed over and categorized as just homelessness. There is no cure for this type of homelessness; it's merely the natural occurrence of an addiction. The only result is revolving door.

Solutions to Getting off the Streets: Transitional Housing, Supportive Housing, and Programs for the Chronic Homeless

Dalton Clark Conley (2006) performed a research study that was meant to point out some of the social and institutional obstacles to getting off the streets in New York. He used this information to determine if the sub cultural dynamic described in the Austin metropolitan area applied to other cities. The institutional obstacles that he found plaguing the homeless the most were dangerousness and unsanitary conditions of city shelters. He found that most of the homeless people he interviewed didn't like staying in the city shelter for too long. Also, about 59.5 percent of the interviewees hadn't even known about a new housing grant that was available (Conley, 2006). He noted that only one of the interviewees claimed that he heard of the housing grant through a caseworker. This is problematic because it raises questions on whether support programs are truly effective. Are the homeless learning of support programs through the proper channels? Socially, Conley pointed out that there is a stigma that follows the homeless and prevents them from being able to obtain jobs and housing. Many have poor hygiene. Employers or landlords don't give them a chance to clean up. Society ultimately distrusts homeless individuals, especially those with a dual diagnosis. In like, the homeless distrust society.

Transitional housing is controversial because while some believe it's a necessary step towards independent living, others feel that it is a drain on the economy and a stigmatizing concept.

There are many types of transitional housing. They include emergency shelters, residential treatment programs, permanent supportive housing, stand-alone programs, including single room occupancy (SRO), and clustered or scattered-site apartments, such as the Young Men's Christian Association (YMCA). High demand transitional housing entails services for those with a mental illness. According to Barrow and Zimmer (2006)

> *Homeless individuals and families troubled by serious mental health and drug abuse problems, domestic violence and HIV/AIDS are among the subgroups whose needs have spurred the development of specialized "high demand" residences.*

However, problems arise under such strict requirements when living in a high demand transitional home. The authors suggest that more research on the effectiveness of these different transitional homes should be conducted.

Alcoholics Anonymous

An interesting phenomenon occurs when a person can successfully break from a revolving door cycle. There are cases where individuals find motivation to end the cycle of institutionalization. The chances are very slim that a person can achieve complete recovery. However, there is another approach to recovery, and it incorporates more support from other individuals. Alcoholics Anonymous (AA) takes on a spiritual approach to getting help from substance abuse. There's a belief that humans need

some sort of foundation that they can trust in order to be lifted from an addiction. Institutions often separate spirituality from therapy. AA holds that if individuals can give themselves diligently and completely to the rules and concepts of the AA testament, then they can break the cycle. However, they must completely surrender to its concepts. Coincidently, most don't surrender completely and often fall out of practice and relapse into a world of drugs. For those with a mental illness, it's even harder to follow the rules of the program (Orange, 2007).

Methodology

General Design

In order to explore the effectiveness of programs designed to help the homeless who are dealing with a dual diagnosis in the Austin metropolitan area, the researcher chose to collect statistics from various studies done in the city that pertain to homelessness rates and mental illness. Also, additional data on reoccurring clients from Institution X was gathered and analyzed. Statistical trends on homelessness throughout the United States were also examined. Additionally, the researcher/observer perused information related to support programs and effective programming. Two case studies and an interview were chosen to support themes that emerged from the data reviewed.

Selection of Cases

Two case studies were examined. The researcher/observer selected a case with a history of dual diagnosis and the tendency to cycle in and out of health clinics. The researcher interviewed the individual with the intentions of analyzing the reasons why people with dual diagnosis end up on the streets. The second case study was chosen to show a different perspective on homelessness and mental illness. The intention of the interview was to try to shed some light on support available in the Austin metropolitan area. This was to in turn answer some questions about the high homelessness rate in this area itself. The interviewee was chosen on the basis that he or she was continuously going in and out of mental health clinics. The case studies included a story of an individual who survived the revolving door cycle and managed to get off the streets and out of homelessness and the other included a study of homelessness within an institution.

Operationalization and Data Collection

The researcher collected data about homelessness from Institution X, the Austin metropolitan area, and other cities in America that are experiencing high rates of homelessness. The case studies and interview were obtained within an AA meeting at Institution X and the unit. The interviewer selected questions that pertained to the following:

- Revolving door syndrome
- Family support
- Effectiveness of institutions
- Effectiveness of support programs
- Spirituality as a means of support within AA

Results

The Case Studies

Michael* came from a wealthy family. He found himself dealing with alcoholism and bipolar disorder. Michael's family didn't want to be bothered with his problems for whatever reasons and refused to give any more help or support. The only natural solution for his problem was to live on the streets. There he continued to cycle in and out of homelessness and temporary housing. Michael exclaimed that people didn't want to have anything to do with him and no one wanted to help. People got tired of giving him money and giving him support. The government wouldn't help and he couldn't claim disability. Michael went through living on the streets and behind dumpsters. One of the things that helped get him sober was when he relapsed and ended up at an institution; he finally realized that no one was going to help him anymore. Michael made the decision to get better, which is what he felt, was an impossible task. Through staying active at AA meetings, he found inspiration in staying sober and off the streets.

Gary*, a client at Institution X, had resided at the institution for about a month. By HUD's definition of homelessness, Gary was homeless because he had lived in an institution for over 30 days and had no family, and lacked the resources necessary for discharge. His diagnosis and symptoms were problematic. Labeled with schizophrenia, Gary seemed to be very disorganized and experienced extreme delusions. Holding an extended conversation with Gary was nearly impossible because his thoughts

56

often drifted into unorganized patterns. It seemed he also had hallucinations because he often talked to people that no one else saw. On the outside it seemed as though Gary was bothered by the voices he heard because he got into a concentration mode where he grabbed his head. Gary will probably always need a high demand of care because therapy techniques and medications didn't seem to work for him.

Analysis of Case Studies

Findings

It is estimated that 3,625 people are homeless in Austin metropolitan area in any given day (Community Partnership for the Homeless, 2003). It is also noted that about 40 percent of the homeless population have a co-existing drug abuse problem and/or mental illness. According to CAN, fifteen percent (15%) of admissions to Institution X were homeless individuals in 2003. It's important to realize that these statistics have increased in the past four years. According to the National Student Campaign Against Hunger and Homelessness (2006), 72% of agencies in Texas reported an increase in food requests and 50% reported an increase in shelter requests from 2003 to 2004. Also, 83% of these agencies reported decreased federal or stagnant funding. Austin and CAN, along with other agencies, are implementing preventative and current plans to alleviate homelessness. Through programs like the Garden Terrace Apartment's supportive housing program (started in 2003 to help the homeless get back on their feet), Austin is trying to make more independent

supportive homes for the homeless, including those with a dual diagnosis.

Through observing the clients that are admitted into Institution X programs seem to be ineffective in that large numbers of clients continue to cycle in and out without breaking out of the revolving door cycle. Through the three months of interning at Institution X, the researcher noted five clients from a particular unit that came back after discharge within two months. This did not include the clients that were relocated to a different unit of care or clients that returned after two months. After talking with qualified staff, they exclaimed that many clients relapsed and came right back into circulation. Also, some clients took advantage of the services for need of detox and getting shelter. After talking to some clients, the researcher concluded that some clients just didn't retain concepts taught in therapy, fell out of interest in taking medications, went back into old habits, lost the ability to maintain personal responsibilities, and of course relapsed. The researcher noted that all of the re-occurring clients were well versed in their illness but struggled with a substance abuse disorder or unsupportive housing.

Relapsing is due to structural and personal situations: lack of good health care, lack of adequate support systems, discrimination, stigmatization, and loss of hope. Most clients said they understood where they could go in the community to get help. One client even said she was homeless before arrival to the institution and agreed that Austin had great homeless shelters. Data on whether Austin is bringing itself out of its homelessness problem is inconclusive due to the lack of research available. However, it was shown that homeless rates in Texas were steadily increasing since 2003. Nationally, homelessness is also increasing. Staff at Institution X have stated that the hospital can only get so much federal funding. There may be other factors contributing to this number including weak programming outside of the institution and unavailability of supportive housing. Homelessness is a complex problem and requires complex solutions to alleviate it. Supportive housing may be more effective for individuals and families that don't suffer from a mental illness and substance abuse problem. Specialized high demand plans for the homeless with a dual diagnosis should be implemented. Michael from the AA meeting explained the two percent rule,

> *Of 100 people that need AA, two of them walk in the doors of AA. Of all that group of 2 percent of people, after 5 years two percent of those are sober. If you tack in mental illness, what's going to happen is that there's going to be nothing but a revolving door.*

This suggests that such a small amount of people ever seek assistance. Out of the people that do seek assistance, only a small amount of them recover from the addiction. This does not include people with a mental illness; it's even harder to recover. However, Michael suggested that even though it's rare that someone fully recovers from an addiction, AA is the best tool we have for addicts. There's just not a more effective program that exists for recovery. It's

rare that people like Gary and Michael recover from homelessness, unless they have sheer determination and constant support. Supportive housing programs show a higher success rate than program methods designed to give shelter, food, and counseling (Barrow & Zimmer, 2006). However, it's difficult to get a homeless person with a dual diagnosis to *want* to change. While some programs are more effective than others, preventative programming on a national level and efficient federal funding need to take place in all cities.

Discussion

Structural causes of homelessness outweigh personal causes. It seems that local agencies understand that the older methods of helping the homeless are less effective because it doesn't attack the problem at its core. Simply giving homeless people temporary food, shelter, and services doesn't alleviate homelessness. In fact, it's a bit more expensive for cities and the nation to do this type of programming (Barrow & Zimmer, 2006). CAN (2003) recommends preventative steps in ending homelessness. Such programming includes: providing adequate services to those who are discharged from state hospitals, help keep families intact, keep children out of foster care, and help people maintain housing and employment. These are all important ways of dealing with homelessness, especially for those with a dual diagnosis.

The support systems and programs in the Austin metropolitan area are not necessarily ineffective. Supportive housing seems to be more effective in ending homelessness than state institutions. However, institutions are definitely not useless. Also, not only do more supportive housing projects need to take place, but the government should get serious about the causes of poverty and homelessness. One hundred and seventy thousand people in metropolitan Austin cannot qualify for GED or job training programs (Literacy Austin, 2006). In 2004, more than 12 percent of Travis County lived below the poverty line (Rasmus, 2006). Housing discrimination against minorities in 2000 was higher in the Austin metropolitan area than the national average (Austin Business Journal, 2006). Tragically, Austin is not the only city that deals with these problems. In some U.S. cities the conditions are worse. For individuals that are living with a dual diagnosis, the condition is even hopeless. Homelessness cannot be cured, but it can be decreased through prevention and national plans to help decrease poverty and homelessness.

References

Austin Business Journal. *Report: Housing Discrimination High in Austin.* 7 November 2002. < http://www.bizjournals.com/austin/stories/2002/11/04/daily49.html >. 4 December 2006.

Barrow, Susan. Zimmer, Rita. *Transitional Housing: A Synthesis.* 4 October 2006. < http://aspe.hhs.gov/homeless/symposium/10.htm >. 4 December 2006.

Bassuk, Ellen L. *The Mental Health Needs of Homeless Persons.* Jossey-Bass Incorporated: San Francisco, 1986.

Burt, Martha. Laudan, Aron. Lee, Edgar. Valente, Jesse. *Helping America's Homeless.* The Urban Institute Press: Washington D.C. 2001.

Community Action Network. *Ending Chronic Homelessness in Austin/Travis County.* December 2003. < http://www.ci.austin.tx.us/budget/beac/downloads/20050926beacpres_echo.pdf >. 4 December 2006.

Community Partnership for the Homeless. *What is Homelessness?* 2003. < http://www.austinhomeless.org/education.html >. 4 December 2006.

Conley, Dalton Clark. *Getting It Together: Social and Institutional Obstacles to Getting Off the Streets.* Sociological Forum, 1996. < www.jstor.org >. 4 October 2006.

Diamond, Pamela M. *Lives in The Shadows: Some of The consequences of a Non-System of Care.* Hogg Foundation For Mental Health: Austin, TX, 1991.

Literacy Austin. *Literacy in Our Community.* < http://www.literacyaustin.org/background.html >. 4 December 2006.

Mechanic, David. Rochefort, David A. *Deinstitutionalization: An Appraisal of Reform.* Annual Reviews, 1990. < www.jstor.org >. 4 October 2006.

National Coalition for the Homeless. *Mental Illness and Homelessness.* NCH fact sheet # 5. June 2006. < www.nationalhomeless.org >. 4 December 2006.

National Student Campaign Against Hunger and Homelessness. www.studentsagainsthunger.org, Retrieved October, 2006.

NPR. *Hard Industry vs. Information Technology.* < http://www.npr.org/templates/story/story.php?storyId=1058125 >. 1999.

Orange, A. *The Effectiveness of the 12 Step Program.* < http://www.orange-papers.org/orange-effectiveness.html > 2007.

Powers, Wayne. *Reversal of Fortune.* < http://www.oprah.com/tows/slide/200612/20061201/slide_20061201_284_108.jhtml >. 2007

Rasmus, Allie. *Austin's Tour of Poverty.* 25 January 2006. Channel 8 News: Top Stories. < http://www.news8austin.com/content/top_stories/?ArID=154391 >. 4 December 2006.

Rassool, Hussein G. *Dual Diagnosis, Substance Misuse and Psychiatric Disorders.* Blackwell Science Incorporated: Malden, MA, 2002.

Siegel, Ronald K. *In Intoxication: Life in Pursuit of Artificial Paradise.* E.P. Dutton, Incorporated: New York, N.Y., 1989.

Shlay, Anne B. Rossi, Peter H. *Social Science Research and Contemporary Studies of Homelessness.* Annual Reviews, 1992. < www.jstor.org >. 17 October 2006.

Sullum, Jacob. *Curing the Therapeutic State: Thomas Szasz Interviewed*

By Jacob Sullum. July 2000. ReasonOnline. < http://www. reason.com/news/show/27767. html >. 4 December 2006.

Texas Homeless Network, Retrieved October, 2006, www.thn.org/ developing_housing_under_coc_ grant.htm.

Wright, Talmadge. *Resisting Homelessness: Global, National, and Local Solutions.* Contemporary Sociology, 2000. < www.jstor.org >. 17 October 2006.

The '80s Babies Cohort: Defining Themes In Paradigmatic Context

Lynn Speed and Kye Tavernier
Seniors, Psychology

(Dr. Debra L. Murphy, Major Advisor for Psychology)

Abstract

This research project explored the defining themes of the "'80s Babies" (those born in the 1980s) within the context of the major psychological paradigms. The research was initiated and carried out by psychology majors in Huston-Tillotson (HT) University's Theories in Psychology class. The students were eighteen to twenty-six years of age (who by definition would be categorized as '80s Babies). The class identified themes pertaining to behavioral and thinking patterns characteristic of this cohort. The class then divided into subgroups to examine each theme within the context of the major psychological paradigms. The subgroups later reconnected as a whole group to compile the findings. The significant impact that family structure had on the '80s Babies generation was found to be a defining theme that could be explained within the context of the major psychological paradigms. The impact of the single parent headed household (usually female) was a point of focus with concern about the decrease in the supportive availability to previous generations of extended family and entire community resources (the village concept). The student researchers identified that lack of attention, and education provided in families were at the root of peers' turning to each other, media generated rap idols, technology (internet games), materialism, (and for some, even gangs, drugs, sex, and violence) for a sense of family, community, self, education, gratification, and life meaning. They cited the source for their feelings of deficient attention from primary family structures as due to distractions that took their parents' quality time away from them and other social problems and factors. These distractions and other social problems and factors included: divorce, never married parents, and/or overworked parent(s); the importation of drugs into the African American Community; the increased incarceration of Black men; the lack of knowledge about African American history (Civil Rights Era, etc.); feelings of inferiority due to constant comparison with Baby Boomers; being conditioned to instant gratification to meet needs promoted by technology and the media; and other issues (some of which are rooted in a lack of opportunity for African Americans). This complex interplay of events was gleaned as the basis of many of the defining themes of the 1980s generation and explainable within existential, sociocultural, cognitive, behavioral, psychodynamic, and African American psychological paradigmatic contexts. Recognition was also expressed about the ability of this generation to use rap, music, fashion, movies, and technology in innovative ways, which could be interpreted as a reflection of its resiliency.

Introduction

Several believed the year 2000 was going to be the end of the world. Life has changed greatly since the Civil Rights Movement. Those who were born in the 1980s have had pretty much everything at their immediate disposal. Technology, education, health issues, and politics, are facets of this generation that have made impacts on the way this age group has chosen to try to find meaning in life and self-actualize.

The altered family structure from two-family headed to single-parent homes, and even no parents at all has resulted in the seeking of role models from other sources: rapper or a video vixen. There is also a focus on individualism, materialism, instant gratification, fame, and acceptance, rather than a focus on unity, generosity, a long life, with prosperity and making sound decisions for the next generation.

Women are not treasured and respected anymore in this period than when it was impossible for them to vote. Men have a loss of confidence and self-esteem, associated with violence and incarceration rates sky rocketing (rooted in discrimination and lack of opportunity for Black males), leaving the youth with the impression that men have no responsibility to families. Drugs have decreased drive and desire, while fostering dependency, plus promoted alternative means of making a living that promote greed and threatening occupations. This disordered state is related to the cohort's fear of failure

and being ridiculed and criticized by peers and society, and contributed to states of self-doubt and cognitive dissonance. However, entrepreneurial routes through rap music, fashion, movies, and technology may reflect resiliency by this generation.

The researchers examined the perspectives of numerous theories in psychology to thoroughly inspect what could be a sufficient reason for how these paradigms relate to the thinking, feelings, and behaviors (the psychology) of the '80s babies generation.

Methodology for the 80's Babies Paradigm

Research for the '80s Babies paradigm was conducted at Huston-Tillotson University (HT) in the fall of 2006 by analyzing how the major psychological theories could explain the '80s Babies generational themes. The researchers (class) used traditional perspectives: Psychoanalytic, Adlerian, Existential/Humanistic, Behavioral, Cognitive, Sociocultural, and nontraditional (African American Psychology) to help describe and understand the '80s babies generational themes. The researchers collected a list of twenty-eight themes that were characteristic of the '80s Babies generation and then used the psychological theories to explain their uniqueness among the '80s Babies cohort:

- Birth
- Teen Pregnancy
- Peer pressure

- Instant Gratification
- Apathy
- Internet
- Media Influence
- Environment
- Divorce
- HIV/AIDS
- Drugs
- Incarceration
- Materialism
- Technology
- Individualism
- Health care
- Education
- Attitude
- Violence
- Music
- Sexuality
- Language
- Education
- Politics
- Lack of role models
- What applied to the '80s Babies generation?
- How do previous generations differ from the 80's Babies?
- What affects their current behaviors and tendencies?
- How does each psychological theory provide insight to the themes of the 80's babies?

The researchers divided into four groups of three; and in the collective groups proceeded to take each generational theme and explain whether or not and how each of the psychological perspectives could explain each of the generational themes. They then reconvened as one focus group to extrapolate common findings from across all of the subgroups to come up with a theoretical framework for understanding, explaining, and predicting behavior for the '80s Babies

generation. The paradigm enhanced their understanding of their generation and many of the problems they face.

Results

Review of Perspectives

Defense mechanisms and unconscious thoughts were the focus from the Psychodynamic Perspective. Family constellation and the search for significance were highlighted from the Adlerian framework. Man's search for meaning was centered on from the Humanistic and Existentialistic perspectives. Modeling, reinforcement, and mental processing were the areas of emphasis from the Behaviorism and Cognitive perspectives. Through the Sociocultural paradigm, social and cultural forces that affect psychology and behavior were emphasized. The unique psychological and behavioral experiences relevant to growing up Black or minority in a majority white culture were focused on from the African American Perspective.

Family Structure

The student self research suggested that much that defines the '80s Babies Cohort is rooted in the increased change in family structure and dynamics due to single female parenthood, divorce, and/or both parents working so hard that their children did not receive the nurturance needed from either immediate or extended family or community as did prior African American generations. The parenting void in their development was replaced by other influences (themselves, their siblings, peers, gangs, rap culture, fashion, materialism, technology and the media, violence, sex, drugs, and/ or incarceration). The changed family structure and dynamics (a focus of the psychodynamic theory put forth by Adler) were expressed as influencing this cohort at many levels beginning in childhood, such as, through feelings of confusion, negligence, trauma, guilt, resentment and anger about divorce, both parents working so hard, and single parenthood (plus possible outgrowths such as poverty or child neglect and abuse) that became embedded in the unconscious mind and continued to influence their behavior for the rest of their lives.

Just as the developmental void was filled too much from outside influences (see above list), there were other coping and defense mechanisms used that included ways to escape through (video games, computers, cell phones, television, and movies, etc.). The quick and easy escape and gratification through technology was also seen as creating a lifelong expectation for instant satisfaction and happiness, which was explainable through reinforcement theory (behaviorism). This was thought to have increased the rate of sexual activity, drug use, and other behaviors (alternative, but often delinquent economies rather than educational pursuits to try to obtain materialistic needs easily rather than through education and/or hard work). Media imagery of divorce, glamorization of commercialized rap, irresponsible sexual behavior, drug use, and instant gratification for materialistic needs through shady alternative economies were seen as providing role modeling and reinforcement (behavioral theory) for this way of thinking and behaving.

This was expressed as leading to many of the defining themes of the '80s Babies Cohort: increased teen pregnancy, HIV/AIDS, gangs and the commercialized rap culture, jail and divorce rates (fear of commitment due to observing their parents' difficulties), which all were thought to have affected this cohort.

Seeking Significance and Meaning of Life

Family structures and dynamics (single female headed household where time was consumed with work and trying to make ends meet and where both parents were working to get ahead or there was disruption due to divorce) were seen to have had a great impact. Also, the media's making it appear that this is alright reinforced this picture. '80s Babies felt a lack of attention and significance and looked for a place to belong and to try to find worth and meaning in their lives (existentialism, humanism, socio-cultural, and psychodynamic perspectives). This was explained as causing '80s Babies to seek attention and places to belong from sources other than the parents, which resulted in siblings or peers raising each other so that the pattern of a life of peer conformity became commonplace. Alternative influences that substituted for families and were often oriented around commercialized rap, materialism, fashion, sex, drugs, violence, and incarceration replaced families as the primary influence. These sort of alternative family structures sometimes caused behaviors that were a part of the commercialized rap culture and/or were glorified by the media. This included stealing or selling drugs for quick and easy financial support, drug abuse to fit in with peers and to escape the feelings of insignificance, too much of a focus on materialism (fashion and *bling bling*) and sex to feel more significant and find meaning in life (existentialism and humanism). This was also explainable as defense mechanisms (psychodynamic theory) that were modeled through and reinforced by the media and the instant gratification that was provided (reinforcement theory). This has also been instilled through technology's quick turnaround of pleasure (for example, game boys).

The instability of familial infrastructures resulting from divorce, separation, never married, and/or both parents having to work may similarly explain the cycle of *baby daddy*, and *baby momma*, drama. Early sexuality and teen pregnancy acceptance was seen as due to the lack of attention within the family. This was thought to have led many girls to unconsciously fill the void and feel significant and complete by seeking the love and support they did not have as a child through sex and having a child (the recipient of fatherhood, himself, possibly not having a role model for fathering and *husbanding* resulting in the cycle continuing). Being a mother enabled girls to give to and receive from babies the attention that they felt they themselves were deprived of. Early sexuality and multiple partners without protection have also been associated with increased rates of STDs/HIV. Males may have sought significance through the commercialized rap lifestyle as a way to find meaning in life and the instant gratification that it provided (sex, having children and

not marrying, drug use and dealing) as opposed to the more prolonged educational route. It was thought that the father figure substitution or greater availability of adult figures in the home could have offset much of this. The prior generations were seen has having the village concept available to supplement (extended familial members and/or community). This was more likely among prior generations (Baby Boomers), but seen as less so given family units currently living much farther away from each other and the African American Community's instability due to families of means moving out of the central part of the city. The media's repeated replaying of the commercialized rap lifestyle was seen as playing a role that reinforced and caused modeling of the *baby momma* and *baby daddy* drama so that it became even more unconsciously implanted as a way to gain attention or significance. It also became more acceptable by the mainstream.

Drug abuse was related to defense mechanisms (psychodynamic) and finding meaning in life (existentialism). Coping with a traumatic environment in the childhood, or subliminal introduction to drugs at an early age may have caused some to find comfort in getting high. The '80s Babies were described as tending to turn to drugs, because of the lack of meaning they felt in their lives, due to the deterioration of the familial structure and the need for immediate gratification and a sense of significance through escape from thoughts of a meaningless life.

Media messages may have subliminally contributed to the high rates of incarceration among '80s Babies. The television replay of young African Americans with incarceration reinforced a sense of unworthiness and stigmatization (subliminal perception). This may have caused some of this cohort to internalize this stigma and the inevitability of jail (a self fulfilling prophecy), which may have enhanced coping by aligning cognitions and reducing anxiety (cognitive dissonance). *Flipping* the interpretation of jail as a source of manhood and a statement of coolness among the commercialized rap culture was subliminally processed and reinforced through media glorification. Delinquency came to represent money, power and/or respect.

Feelings of meaninglessness contributed to lives of crime and violence, which were modeled and reinforced socially through family, peers, and the gang lifestyle, as well as, through technology (video games, music, television, movies, and the internet) so that it became acceptable. The '80s Babies Cohort became desensitized to the pain and hurt associated with violence and through models in their environment, began to use and respect violence as a way to demand respect to make them feel significant.

Self-expression through the rap, technology, and fashion culture and industries was explained as a way for this cohort to disassociate themselves from a sense of meaninglessness felt within their family and community contexts. Having the latest iPod or cell phone fulfilled desires to belong among peers and be recognized. Materialism among this generation through fashion and *bling bling* provided self-worth.

Life's meaning became based on the status associated with materialism (flashy cars, fine clothes, and expensive jewelry). Influential people (Puff Daddy, Beyonce' and other cultural icons) reinforced and classically conditioned these messages through music, movies, television and other technology.

Out of the Box

The '80s Babies Cohort was interpreted as having *flipped the script* (defense mechanism) in many ways, such as, commercializing their perceived life struggles and reversing language terminology, which have become a part of mainstream culture. The '80s Babies witnessed the commercial successes of their icons selling their life stories (perceptions of childhood and socio-cultural conflicts and trauma and their connection with striving for meaning and significance in life through music, fashion, and technology). These new career paths were used to find success (strive for superiority) and compensate for feelings of inferiority (Psychodynamic/Adlerian). They were perceived as a more instant route to gratification (which technology had conditioned them to) than education's prolonged educational route.

Not having money to go to college or even try, when as much or more money can be made through other routes were used to rationalize not pursuing education. Mental defenses explained the devaluing of educational pursuits to the preference for more immediately gratifying commercialized rap economies (drugs and sex, for some). The influence of striving for superiority rooted in feeling inferior from growing up without resources in a materialistic society that is blasted into minds through the media day in and day out was thought to be very significant in defining the '80s Babies.

The increased rate of perceived inappropriate language use by '80s babies was strongly defended. They rationalized the popular use of the "n" word and the "b" word as empowerment through their rebellion against norms by flipping of their meanings from negative to positive. They felt (as have some in generations before them, e.g. Dick Gregory, Whoopie Goldberg, Richard Pryor, and others) that this stripped the words of their historically negative power (a mental defense mechanism) and like dialects and generational slang, provided social significance, meaning, and recognition (Adlerian, existentialistic, and African American perspectives).

Politics

Their unconscious perceptions of powerlessness to make a difference explained lack of political involvement. Parents were described as sending mixed messages. They were said to have bragged and glorified their '60s activism, but did not educate and equip their kids ('80s Babies) with the history to instill political empowerment and activism. They unconsciously processed that they could not measure up to Baby Boomers. The '80s Babies Cohort has focused on *getting mine* (individualistic goals) as a result of their parents not wanting them to experience the same scars that they did

from fighting the system through group activism.

The '80s Babies associated politics with lies and corruption (for instance, the Florida Recount of 2000). This reduced their desire to commit to political and social interest (Psychodynamic/ Adlerian Theory). The perception of voting not mattering reinforced unconscious apathy. Society's lack of acknowledgement of African American/minority opinion fostered feelings of meaninglessness and a lack of faith in the educational and political systems.

Discussion

The '80s Babies paradigmatic analysis attempted to explain how the various psychological theories can elucidate the generation's issues to increase understanding of their behavior and thinking. The '80s Babies researchers analyzed the relationship of their generational themes to the Psychodynamic, Existentialistic, Humanistic, Behavioral, Cognitive, Socio-cultural, and African American Perspectives.

The lack of attention to children resulting from divorce, separation, single motherhood, and/or parents working too hard was a recurring theme. Teen pregnancy was explained by the psychodynamic perspective as associated with repressed feelings from father absence that were manifested as attention seeking from males; an outgrowth of which may explain the STD/HIV rate. Further, reference was made to an alternative view that the father absence experience, but *strong mother presence* compensation, may have made children more resilient as a result of all that they have had to overcome.

The family structure disintegration due to divorce, separation, or single motherhood resulted in youth having to raise each other (via siblings, peers, and or gangs). Meaning in life (existentialism) was sought from outside forces (peers, commercialized rap, fashion, technology, gangs, drugs, and sex) and reinforced through media imagery and popularization of the commercialized rap culture. This was explained by cognitive and behavioral perspectives. The easy money and gratification projected by the media of the commercialized rap culture (the rap and fashion industries) promoted finding significance in life through these venues rather than the delayed gratification of education (high school and college). The glamorization of incarceration became a reinforced deviant behavior associated with the rap culture (behaviorism). Commercialized rap and its associated industries (fashion and technology) helped to reinforce a market where '80s Babies could package and sell their perceived hard lives for the instant gratification of fast hard money (behaviorism) that helped them to feel validated (existentialism).

This presented economic alternatives to the more delayed gratification and collective concerns of their Baby Boomer parents, who they faulted with not providing the historical knowledge of and tools for activism. Instead, the life circumstances for '80s Babies promoted the desire for individualistic prosperity reinforced by the commercialized rap culture that has become mainstream. The '80s Babies pride themselves with continuing the legacy of the African American entrepreneurial spirit through economic alternatives to those that are education-focused. They have disempowered words that humiliated prior generations (Baby Boomers). The '80s Babies consider this a form of activism. They developed life meaning out of negligence due to family structures and/or both parents working through alternative family structures (peers, gangs, drugs, sex, commercialized rap, and fashion).

The results and findings of this theoretical compilation model were limited to the researchers' internal focus group. They cannot be generalized to the population of '80s Babies at large. Future studies may want to include more diverse samples of this cohort, including different socio-economic backgrounds, as well as members in different major areas of study at Huston-Tillotson University.

References

Comer, Ronald J. (2007). *Abnormal Psychology* (6th Ed.). New York, NY: Worth.

Jones, Reginald L. (1991). *Black Psychology* (3rd Ed.) Berkeley, California.

Shultz, Duane, Schultz, Sydney Ellen. (1998), *Theories of Personality* (6th Ed.). Pacific Grove, CA. Brooks/ Cole Publishing Company

Weiten, W. *Psychology Themes and Variations: Briefer Version,* (7th Edition), Las

Vegas, Nevada. Thomson-Wadsworth, 2008, 304-337.

Powell, Alfred, and Marie, Donna (2006), *Hip Hop Hypocrisy: When Lies Sound Like the Truth.*

iUniverse. Bloomington, Indiana.

II. Historical Research Papers & Research Abstracts and Posters

Figure 1
Restoration of a Safe Place
King's Eulogy for the Martyred Children

Matthew L. Morris
Senior, History

(Dr. Janice Sumler-Edmond, Major Advisor for History)

Dr .Martin Luther King delivered a Eulogy for four the little girls who had been killed in a church bombing. King's charge was not only to bring comfort to the families of these slain children, but to restore a community and remind them of hope. The church is seen as a safe haven for many and to know such a catastrophic event could take place in a sacred edifice had to have been devastating to one's faith.

Birmingham, Alabama in 1963 could be seen as one of the major hotbeds for civil injustice in the South. Jim Crow laws, segregation, and other racist events were the norm for that day. Being black might often mean that you were also a target. African Americans had begun to take a stand against these injustices, but those protests did not sit well with the majority of the white South. Black southerners began to organize through such groups as the Southern Christian Leadership

Conference (SCLC), the Student Nonviolent Coordinating Committee (SNCC), and the Congress of Racial Equality (CORE). These groups used different tactics, mostly centered on civil disobedience, to protest and demand their god-given rights as citizens of the United States and as human beings. Although these groups strove towards non-violence their oppressors did not partake in this tactic; African Americans who got involved with the movement knew the cost and the ultimate sacrifice that they must be willing to make, life.

Figure 2

On Sunday September 15, 1963, Addie Mae Collins age fourteen, Denise McNair age eleven, Carole Robertson age fourteen, and Cynthia Wesley age fourteen were attending service at the Sixteenth Street Baptist Church in Birmingham. Between Sunday school and morning worship an act would transpire that would shock and appall the nation, letting America know that change was quickly needed. Around 10:30 a.m. on that day the Sixteenth Street Baptist church was bombed, many people were injured but the aforementioned girls became martyrs for the movement. Their lives were taken not because they had done wrong, but because they were attending a black church that was a target of segregationists.

Figure 3

Three of the families of these children decided to have the funeral together and Rev. Martin Luther King, Jr. was chosen to do the eulogy. By 1963 Dr. King had become a renowned leader of the civil rights movement; just a month prior to the murder of the young girls in Alabama, Dr. King had delivered his *I Have a Dream* speech at the March on Washington. In this speech he gave a message of hope, love, and freedom. Dr. King was then the head of SCLC; founded in January of 1957 at Ebenezer Baptist Church in Atlanta, GA. SCLC's first initiative was a Crusade for Citizenship which included leadership training programs and citizen education projects.

Figure 4

King began humbly, the son of a black Baptist preacher in Atlanta, Georgia. As a young man, King succeeded in his education. In June of 1949 Martin Luther King, Jr. graduated from Morehouse College with a degree in Sociology. He also attended Crozer Theological Seminary where he studied about Mahatma Gandhi and his non-violent techniques. King continued his educational career and earned a Ph.D. from Boston University. After graduation King moved to Montgomery, Alabama and was installed as the pastor of Dexter Avenue Church. As the newest leader in town, King was placed on the forefront of the civil rights movement. This was the beginning of an eloquent crusade to fight injustices throughout the Southern United States. Along with the protests came bombs, threats, jail, and untimely death yet King remained steadfast even to a point to where he was able to publish several books and maintain numerous speaking engagements. King faced a number of challenges during 1963. "When in the first week of April

1963, Dr. Martin Luther King moved to challenge Birmingham's segregation fortress from the inside, it was like Daniel walking into the lion's den" (Mendelsohn, 1966).

For King and numerous other black southerners, the church played a major role in their lives. He obtained his license in 1947 and was ordained 1948 as a minister in the Baptist Church. Although attacked, chastised, and beaten throughout the week, Sundays could always be seen as a time of renewal. The Protestant denomination, in the black community, is forefront with a focus on Methodist and Baptist Churches. The *black church* has often focused on social issues of unemployment, poverty, and racism. The church also provided a means of social support and even an aid in dealing with alcoholism or other addictions.

On Sunday September 15, 1963 the members of Sixteenth Street Baptist Church came together to celebrate youth Sunday. Cynthia Wesley was the daughter of a proud Claude A. Wesley, the fifty-four year old principal of a Negro school. Her mother was a school teacher. Cynthia was an only child and on that morning her mother was not feeling well. As a result her father undertook the Sunday morning routine of making bacon, eggs, and coffee. Cynthia went to her room, put on a ruffled white dress and a red sweater and then went back to the kitchen to feed her pet cocker spaniel. A little after 10 a.m. she and her father pulled up to the church and her father affectionately gave Cynthia a send-off pat on the shoulder as she slid out of the front seat. He said, "You go in honey, and

I'm going to get some gas and be back in a minute" (Mendelsohn, 1966).

Meanwhile Denise McNair, the daughter of Chris and Maxine, both graduates of Tuskegee Institute, began her Sunday morning routine putting on a brand new winter cotton purple dress. Denise loved to dance, play piano, and read books. She was extremely creative. There was a point when she became disappointed that most of the people she read about were white so she decided to write her own short story with characters that reflected all types of children, not just white. That morning the family went to their own designated places of worship. Chris who was Lutheran was picked up by his cousin and went to St. Paul's which was about two miles away from Sixteenth Street Church. Meanwhile Maxine and her daughter went on their way to service not knowing this would be their final moments together. Once at the church Maxine went to her Sunday school class which was held in the choir loft after making sure her daughter made it to her class in the basement.

Carole Robertson, was one of three children. Her father was a well known band teacher, and her mother was a community leader who was also was well known throughout Birmingham. Along with playing in the Parker High Band, Carole was active in Girl Scouts and an organization started by her mother entitled Jack & Jill, Inc. These three girls had known a life of material comfort, yet the struggle of being black in Birmingham was not limited to social class. Addie Mae, the fourth girl had known poverty, she grew up in a rather large family. Also a member of the band, Addie Mae was a good student, active, popular, and ready to serve with the other three girls as ushers for morning worship.

The theme for that Sunday was *The Love that Forgives* with scriptural support found in the fifth chapter of Matthew: 43-44, which reads "Ye have heard that it hath been said, Thou shalt love thy neighbor, and hate thine enemy. But I say unto you, Love your enemies, bless them that curse you, do good to them that hate you, and pray for them which despitefully use you, and persecute you." This message is one that Jesus Christ has preached to a multitude of people about how to love those that hate you and do wrong unto you, a message that would serve the congregation well later that same day.

"At 10:22 am, Claude Wesley stood with the attendant who was filling his car's gas tank at a service station two blocks from the church. All at once the whole morning exploded. At St. Paul's, Chris McNair also heard the blast, but thought it was thunder. Soon there was a phone call telling the worshipers at the Lutheran church what happened" (Mendelsohn 1966).

Figure 5

The bombing, the deadliest single act during the Civil Rights Movement, revealed the growing hostility of segregationists toward the campaign for equal rights in the south. The Sixteenth Street Church had been a center for civil rights organizing and was serving that function at the time, trying to desegregate Birmingham schools. The city had suffered eleven other bombings the previous six months, living up to the nickname Bombingham that it had earned in the 1950's (Carson, 2003).

In a 2005 article by National Public Radio (NPR) Carolyn McKinstry recollects the events that transpired that September day, here is her story.

The bomb exploded mid-morning, during Sunday services. Carolyn McKinstry, who was 14 years old at the time, was secretary of her Sunday school class. She was taking attendance records into the sanctuary when the bomb went off. I heard something that sounded, at first, a little like thunder and then just this terrific noise and the windows came crashing in. It was no accident that the Ku Klux Klan targeted the 16th Street Baptist Church. It was the largest black church in Birmingham, but because of its central location it was used for a lot of other things, all kinds of meetings, national, local and so forth. The Byzantine-style structure, with two domed towers and a roomy basement auditorium, served as the hub for the mass meetings of the civil rights movement, drawing leaders like Martin Luther King Jr. Marchers would assemble at the church and then cross the street to demonstrate at Kelly Ingram Park, the site of violent clashes between Birmingham police and civil rights activists. "These are friends of mine,' and we come to Sunday school one day and they're gone. They're dead. They're just blown away and Birmingham goes on with business as usual." (http://www.npr.org/templates/story/story.php?storyId=1431932).

Carolyn McKinstry gave a first hand account of the dramatic event. She was the same age as the young girls who died and was so close to being a fifth victim of the bomb.

Reverend Connie Lynch, a white supremacist from Birmingham stated, "The victims weren't children. Children are little people, little human beings, and that means white people.... They're just little niggers, and if there's four less niggers tonight, then I say, "Good for whoever planted the bomb" (Carson, 2003). "This statement embodies the racism that was found in Birmingham after the bombing. When a man is full of racial hatred and knows how to use dynamite, he can be dangerous. Dynamite costs little; is easy to obtain, and planting it under the cover of darkness requires no valor, only a modest amount of shrewdness. When the charge goes off, stewing rubble and death; there are no fingerprints to implicate suspects, no slugs or pellets to be sent to a ballistics laboratory" (Mendelsohn, 1966). From the year of 1947 to 1963 more than fifty bombings were accredited to racial extremist (not counting those which were overlooked); of those not one had been solved by 1963.

The fact remains that four girls were slain as a result of prejudice and discrimination. Dr. Martin Luther King, Jr. was charged to eulogize three of these girls. The family of Carole Robertson declined to participate in the mass funeral service held for the other children. King was unable to attend Carol's service, which was held a day prior to the other girls, but he did send a message by way of Rev. Fred Shuttlesworth. The messages read, "This child's life constitutes a sacrifice upon the altar of honor." Reverend

John Cross, the pastor of Sixteenth Street delivered Carole's eulogy, and he said, "To question the rightness of Carole's death was to question the power, sovereignty, and majesty of God, who can bring light from darkness, good from evil, and order from disorder " (Mendelsohn, 1966). By accepting what God allowed to happen that September day, the citizens of Birmingham realized the severity of the race problem and they began to look for a solution.

The next day Dr. King delivered a eulogy for the three remaining girls. Like Rev. Cross he placed emphasis on the wonders of God. His message was one of hope and using the opportunity to learn and continue to strive for freedom. In front of a crowd of well over 4,000 people Kings used vivid imagery to begin to heal the hearts broken by this tragedy. He stated, "These children-unoffending; innocent and beautiful were the victims of one of the most vicious, heinous crimes ever perpetrates against humanity. Yet they died nobly." King recognized the innocence of these children and lets us know that their death is not in vain. "The loss of these children means that silence is no longer an option. The blast from the bomb must be felt all around the world in every facet of human life from the pulpit to politics these children's death will not be pushed aside like so many others who are not seen in the history books. "

King used scripture to support his strong words, thus appealing to the 'black church' and bringing out a justification of peace. King also appealed to the members of the black church by reminding them that "Christianity's affirmation that death is not the end. Death is not a period that ends the great sentence of life, but a comma that punctuates to a more lofty significance. With all the words of comfort that are given at the time of grief, this statement alone reminds the church of hope, for they believe that to die in the Lord is gain, thus there is no need for people to be afraid of death or what may happen in the years to come."

Hearts came together in such sad times. On the day of the funeral SNCC workers tried to come together and protest. They were urged by King to stop. He told them that a funeral was not the time or place for a demonstration. A demonstration would not honor the lives of the four children. There still remained a need for restoration in the hearts and minds of the people in the South. With the death of these four girls a hole had been placed in the hearts of many. King's words began to heal that wound, but a scar would remain to remind the people never to forget. It took well over thirty years for all of the men accused of this crime to get punished, yet the wound still remains. To have four innocent girls ripped from life due to the color of their skin was and is appalling. Healing and restoration began with the words of Dr. King, "So they did not die in vain... Goodnight sweet princesses; may the flight of angels take thee to thy eternal rest."

Works Cited

Carson, Clayborne. Civil Rights Chronicle: *The African American Struggle for Freedom.* Legacy Publishing, 2003.

Mendelsohn, Jack. *The Martyrs: Sixteen who gave their lives for racial Justice.* New York: Harper & Row Publishers, 1966.

Sobel, Lester A. *Civil Rights: 1960-1966.* New York: Facts on File Inc.,1967

Other Sources Used

Carson, Clayborne. *The Autobiography of Martin Luther King Jr.* New York: Warner Brooks, 1998.

King, Coretta Scott. *My Life with Martin Luther King, Jr.* New York: Holt, Rinehart, and Winston, 1969.

King, Martin. *The Trumpet of Conscience.* New York: Harper and Row, 1967.

Lincoln, Eric C. *Martin Luther King, Jr. A Profile.* New York: Hill and Wang, 1970.

Morris, Aldon D. *The Origins of the Civil Rights Movement: Black Communities Organizing for Change.* New York: The Free Press, 1984.

Powledge, Fred. *Free at Last? The Civil Rights Movement ad the People who Made it.* New York: HarperPerennial, 1991.

*Images from::http://search.aol.com/aol/image?invocationType=rboxImgDtls&query=Birmingham%20Bombing%20Martin%20Luther%20King&icid=snap-pic&flv=1

Abstracts and Posters (2007)

Global Warming: Prevention and Reduction

Richard Northcote
Junior, Chemistry
(Dr. Muchere Russ, Major Advisor for Chemistry)

Global warming is a major environmental issue in the United States and worldwide. Global warming is the result of radiative forcing from solar radiation. The radiative forcing can cause heating if it becomes trapped or cooling if it is reflected. Anthropogenic CO_2 is a major contributor of global warming. Historically, CO_2 levels have followed a fluctuating pattern between ice ages and warm temperatures. As CO_2 production levels rise, deforestation globally has been increasing. Discussion of the effects of global warming/cooling from CO_2 related sources will also meet with ways of countering global warming. Global cooling will also be addressed with the effects of Biogenic Volatile Organic Compounds (BVOC) creating radiation repelling aerosols and cloud condensing nuclei (CCN). CCN causes cloud density to increase and to reduce the amount of solar radiation reaching earth's surface. Forested areas are a large source of BVOCs. Therefore the suggestion is placed forward that increased forestation could decrease the effects of CO_2 and also further cool the earth surface temperature.

Cigarettes: Their Chemicals and Their Effects

Alexander Rancier
Senior, Chemistry and Biology
(Dr. Muchere Russ, Major Advisor for Chemistry)

Tobacco use remains a leading preventable cause of death in the United States, resulting in an average of 444,000 premature deaths per year. Cigarettes contain over 600 ingredients and 4,000 chemicals, many of which are toxic, carcinogenic, and mutagenic. The mainstream and side stream smoke that is emitted from the end of the cigarette is responsible for the harmful effects to people. A group of compounds contained in cigarettes, know as tobacco specific nitrosamines (TSNAs), have been proven to cause cancer. The goal of this research is to investigate TSNAs, nitro-pesticides, and other compounds in cigarettes to thoroughly evaluate and exhibit through research what harm a cigarette can truly cause. The analytical methods used to analyze cigarette smoke will be discussed.

Robotics
Idali Hernandez
Senior, Computer Science
(Dr. Hershall Shelley, Major Advisor for Computer Science)

The Height of the Civil Rights Movement: Birmingham, Alabama-1963
Jarrett Kinley-Foster, Matthew L. Morris (Junior, History),
Damien Wooley (Senior, Business), **Christine Henderson**
(Sophomore, Business)
(Dr. Janice Sumer-Edmond, Major Advisor for History)

Four students from History 383-African American History II (fall semester 2006) researched and chronicled the major events, themes and personalities that collectively characterized the civil rights crusade in Birmingham, Alabama, during 1963. Four themes were examined using a timeline, brief descriptive narratives and photographs.

Theme 1--*A Struggle for Peace: Dr. King's Letter from a Birmingham Jail- April 1963:*

Dr. King outlined his strategy for correcting injustice in the South with four basic steps of a non-violent campaign.

Theme 2--*The "Race" for Justice and Equality*: What concepts and tools did Dr. King and Mr. Eugene "Bull" Connor use in their "race" to influence the hearts and minds of the people of Birmingham and the nation?

Theme 3--*An Analysis: the Nightmare on Sixteenth Street in Birmingham*: During September 1963, a bomb destroyed a church and killed four black girls. What was the genesis of that hateful act, and how did Dr. King and others propose to make changes?

Theme 4—*"Love that Forgives"—Restoration of a Safe Place:* Who were the four girls who died in the Sixteenth Street Baptist Church? What is their legacy and how was the church (and the community) restored to safety following the bombing?

Student Learning is Maximized Through Lessons That Support Multiple Intelligences

Ileana Zea-Hernandez Senior, Biology

(Dr. Muchere Russ, Major Advisor for Chemistry,)

Only 75% of Texas students met the Grade 11 TAKS Science standards in Spring 2006. I believe students learning will increase when teachers present science lessons that support auditory, visual and kinesthetic learning styles. This research paper explores my hypothesis that science lessons that support visual, auditory and kinesthetic learning styles are more effective than lessons that only support one learning style. This paper will also review three specific lessons in biology that support these three learning styles. Future classrooms in Texas may use these lessons to reinforce the Grade 11 TAKS Science objective (structures and properties of matter). This objective is the focus of the lessons because it was the least met objective on the Spring 2006 TAKS Science test with only 58% of students passing.

Newborn Screening for Genetic Disorders

Ne'Cole Brinkley

Junior, Chemistry

(Dr. Muchere Russ, Major Advisor for Chemistry)

Newborn screening identifies early conditions that can lead to tragic health problems and/or death. The Texas Newborn Screening Program (NBS) currently screens for 5 disorders and will increase to 27 disorders in April of 2007.The purpose of this study is to understand how the specific testing is conducted and the rationale and probable effectiveness of this increase in screening. The goals of the Texas NBS Program are to ensure that (1) each baby born in Texas receives two newborn screening test; the first within the first 72 hours of life and the second test at one to two weeks of age. (2) All infants testing outside of normal limits of a newborn screening condition receive prompt and appropriate confirmatory testing, and (3) all individuals diagnosed with newborn screening conditions are maintained on appropriate medical therapy. The current five state mandated disorders are CH-Congenital hypothyroidism, H-HPE- Benign Hyperphenylalaninemia, PKU- Phenylketonuria, HEAR- Hearing, and GALT-Transferase deficient galactosemia. A more detailed presentation on the blood cell disorder, Sickle Cell Disease and two inborn errors of amino acid metabolism: PKU- Phenylketonuria, and MSUD- Maple Syrup Urine Disease. Some of these and other more prevalent disorders and the testing method are covered.

Abstracts and Posters (2008)

Auditory and Visual Influence on the Vestibular System

Daena Maxwell, Senior Kinesiology

(Dr. Rozena McCabe, Major Advisor for Kinesiology)

The purpose of this research was to determine whether auditory and visual feedback had an influence on the vestibular system. To determine this, a series of trials were conducted on a random group of fifteen participants all over the age of eighteen. The experiment included a controlled trial with the participants using available feedback from visual and auditory system, three trials included the participants losing feedback from each system (auditory and visual), and finally feedback from both systems were removed. The results support the idea that auditory and visual feedbacks have a significant influence on the proper function of the vestibular system.

Effects of Mental and Physical Rehearsal on Motor Performance

Lovetta Gibson, Senior Kinesiology/Psychology

(Dr. Rozena McCabe, Major Advisor for Kinesiology)

Mental rehearsal is thinking about or mentally imaging certain aspects of the skills being learned, without engaging in any kind of actual movement. Hence numerous athletes are turning towards mental preparation to take their performance to the next level. This research examines if mental practice promotes skill acquisition. Data was collected with two groups (mentally rehearsed and physically practiced) using the Minnesota Manual Dexterity Test, to measure coordination in a timed condition. The statistical analysis indicates that the time needed to perform the task decreased with both groups in each condition. Both groups showed an increase in performance. However, the physical practice group showed a larger increase in performance than the mental rehearsal group. This result could be caused by the initial time disparity during the pre-test between the two groups. As a performer strives to gain skill, mental imagery seems to be an effective mechanism to support further development. The benefits of mental imagery have indicated success at any level. This also specifies that mental imagery can improve physical performance.

Metal Production via Electrolysis

Edward Kozel, Junior Mathematics

(Dr. Muchere Russ, Major Advisor for Chemistry)

Electrolysis is the most efficient method for separating metals from salts or mixtures. The theory of electrolysis, Downs cell, Hall-Heroult process, and electroplating are discussed. Advantages and disadvantages of each cell/process are included.

Nuclear Energy and Nuclear Reactors

Crystal Jackson, Junior Chemistry

(Dr. Muchere Russ, Major Advisor for Chemistry)

The design factors of water and breeder nuclear reactors are reviewed. The implications of the design as well as the nuclear fission and fusion are discussed. Safety issues are also covered.

HT National Science Teachers Association Student Chapter Earth Day Focus

NSTA Student Chapter (Phylliss McKissick, Daria Godfrey, Shayla Yarbrough)

[Drs. Jenefred Davies (Education) and Muchere Russ (Chemistry)]

The chapter celebrated Earth Day by preparing a poster and table complete with tree quiz, chapter information, and Austin poster giveaways.

AFTERWORD

These extremely insightful works by some of HT's finest students were written before President Barack Hussein Obama's historic and (what some might characterize as) oxymoronic election. The articles address connected themes of existentialism, humanism, social consciousness, self empowerment, and generational differences in worldviews, which have been used to describe the Obama campaign. While Alvarez, Hernandez, Ormsby, and Garza highlighted gaps in the system pertaining to "marginalized" populations and the need for improved treatment of the "institutionalized," they presented constructive recommendations that reflected hopefulness in the human spirit, and this country's willingness to meet its human rights obligations to "the least of these." Social, health (Rancier and Brinkley), educational (Zea-Hernandez), and environmental (Northcote) justice issues permeate these authors' works, which is contrary to the egocentric stereotype of their generation. Speed and Tavernier's soul searching analysis of their own generation ('80s Babies) within a social, psychological, historical, and political paradigm challenged whether Baby Boomer parents have met their obligation to show the next generation the way of social consciousness and activism. They highlighted that cohort differences may be more a function of "miseducation" and misunderstandings than gaps, which was similarly echoed by Blackmon's ethnographic exploration of youth perceptions of morality. Morris's work poignantly rounds this journal out. His retrospective on the Birmingham Bombing tragic loss of life that resulted in an improvement of it for the next generation, places the worldview of those born in the 1960s squarely within a context that subsequent generations can understand. This is analogous to the desegregation movement's culmination in the presidency of Obama. There is a common thread throughout these articles that is consistent with his call for a renewed invigoration of the spirit of hopefulness and social justice. Yes we can.

Debra L. Murphy, Ph.D., M.P.H., Professor of Psychology

Journal Editor

Special Acknowledgements:

The students who participated in Research Day
Johnson Controls
The Huston-Tillotson University
Student Research Day Committee 2007-2008
Dr. Muchere Russ, Chair
Dr. Michelle Aynesworth
Dr. Ardavan E-Lotfalian
Dr. Carolyn Golden
Dr. Robert L. Kellogg
Dr. Joseph Jones, ex officio
Dr. Debra L. Murphy, Journal Editor
Advisors for Student Publications
Education, Dr. Jenefred Davies
Kinesiology, Dr. Rozena McCabe
Psychology, Dr. Debra L. Murphy
Chemistry and Biology, Dr. Muchere Russ
Computer Science, Dr. Hershall Shelley
History, Dr. Janice Sumler-Edmond
Supported by:
Johnson Controls

HUSTON-TILLOTSON
UNIVERSITY